William Henry Withrow

The Romance of Missions

William Henry Withrow

The Romance of Missions

ISBN/EAN: 9783744772211

Printed in Europe, USA, Canada, Australia, Japan

Cover: Foto ©ninafisch / pixelio.de

More available books at **www.hansebooks.com**

DR. COKE.
The Father of Methodist Missions.

THE ROMANCE OF MISSIONS.

BY THE
REV. W. H. WITHROW, M.A.

> QUIS JAM LOCUS, . . .
> QUÆ REGIO IN TERRIS . . NON PLENA LABORIS?
> VIRG. ÆN. LIB. I. VV. 463, 464.

TORONTO:
SAMUEL ROSE, METHODIST BOOK ROOM.
1879.

ENTERED, according to the Act of Parliament of Canada, in the year one thousand eight hundred and seventy-nine, by the Rev. WILLIAM H. WITHROW, M.A., in the Office of the Minister of Agriculture.

TO THE

REV. SAMUEL ROSE, D.D.,

WHO, IN EARLY LIFE,

BY HIS OWN MINISTERIAL LABOURS,

HAS ILLUSTRATED

THE ROMANCE OF MISSIONS,

This Book,

AS A TRIBUTE OF ESTEEM AND AFFECTION,

IS

RESPECTFULLY DEDICATED

BY

THE AUTHOR.

CONTENTS.

	PAGE
I. THE CONVERSION OF BRITAIN	1
II. ST. BONIFACE, THE APOSTLE OF GERMANY	30
III. THE CONVERSION OF NORWAY AND SWEDEN	43
IV. THE CONVERSION OF RUSSIA AND PRUSSIA	60
V. RAYMOND LULLI, THE MARTYR OF TUNIS	72
VI. THE MARTYRS OF CANADA	88
VII. DR. COKE, THE FATHER OF METHODIST MISSIONS	118

PREFACE.

No sphere of human endeavour has furnished scope for nobler heroism than that of Christian missions. No work is more instinct with the spirit of our holy religion than mission work. No theme brings us more closely in contact with the noble army of martyrs and confessors for Jesus. Through the ages and in many lands they bore testimony to the truth, often sealing it with their blood.

Several of the examples of missionary faith and zeal here given are of men who lived and died before the era of the Protestant Reformation. For this it is felt that no apology is needed. "It is well for the Protestant of to-day," writes Dr. Whedon, "occasionally to go back on the path of history, and form frseh acquaintance with the men of God who lightened up the night of the distant past. It intensifies our feeling of human brotherhood. It gives us a salutary consciousness of our communion with the Church general in all times and nations and sects. The chain of saints is a chain which stretches through *all* the ages."

The present is an age of greatly revived and extended missionary enterprise. The purpose of these pages is to quicken the sympathies of their readers with this grandest of causes. May the examples of the holy men, whose lives are here recorded, be an inspiration to duty in promoting the object for which they nobly lived and grandly died!

W. H. W.

TORONTO, March 1st, 1879.

THE ROMANCE OF MISSIONS.

THE CONVERSION OF BRITAIN

"GO ye into all the world and preach the Gospel to every creature," was the mandate of the risen Saviour to the little band of unlearned and ignorant men who had been His disciples. And these Galilean peasants boldly assayed the gigantic task, enbraved by the words of their Master, "All power is given unto me in heaven and in earth. . . And lo! I am with you alway, even to the end of the world." In a few brief years, therefore, in all the great centres of ancient civilization and heathen culture—in Egypt, Syria, Asia Minor, Greece, Italy, and Gaul —the new evangel was proclaimed. The seed of the kingdom was becoming a mighty tree, whose leaves were for the healing of the nations. Even in remotest regions, the Man of Nazareth, who, in an obscure Syrian tetrarchate, had lived a life of poverty and died a death of shame, was honoured and adored as very God. "We are but of yesterday," writes Tertullian, at the close of the second century, "yet we fill every town, city, and island of the Empire. Even those places in Britain, hitherto inaccessible to the Romans, have been conquered by Christ."

The names of those early missionaries who first carried the Gospel to the ends of the earth, are lost in glorious obscurity. Unrecorded on earth, they are written in the Lamb's Book of Life. The tomb of Saint Thomas, indeed, is shown on the Malabar coast, and Saint Paul is said to have visited Great Britain; but these legends rest on unverifiable traditions. Probably some of the "strangers of Rome" who witnessed the miracle of Pentecost, or, perhaps, the Gentile converts of the "Italian band" of Cornelius, brought the new evangel to their native city. Certain it is, that as early as A.D. 58 the faith of Roman Church was "spoken of throughout the whole world." It is probable that Christian soldiers or civilians accompanied the Roman armies that invaded Britain. The Claudia mentioned by Saint Paul in the year A.D. 66, it is generally admitted, was the daughter of a British king.

The venerable Bede asserts that in the second century the meek religion of Jesus had supplanted the bloody rites of the Druids throughout Britain; but he adds the incredible legend that a hierarchy of twenty-eight bishops and three archbishops was established in the island. The last of the ten terrible persecutions—that of Diocletian—was felt even in Britain. The first British martyr was Alban of Verulam. During the persecution he gave shelter to a Christian presbyter who was a fugitive from slaughter. He even exchanged clothes with his guest, and was apprehended in his stead. He boldly avowed himself a Christian, and had the honour of becoming the first of the glorious bead-roll of Christ's martyr's in Britain, A.D. 303. Constantine the Great, who was proclaimed Emperor at York, A.D. 306, and who, soon after, made Christianity the religion of the Roman Empire, built a church in honour of the martyr, around which grew up in course of time the monastery of which the ruins still remain, and the town of St. Alban's in Hertfordshire.

In the fourth and fifth centuries the Arian heresy, which was so triumphant in the West, prevailed, according to the testimony of Gildas, one of the earliest monkish historians, extensively in Britain. The heretical opinions of Pelagius, who appears to have been a native of Ireland, were also widely diffused by his disciples and fellow-countrymen. The symbols of religion had, however, degenerated into battle cries, and in their conflict with the Picts the Britons advanced to the charge with warlike shouts of "Hallelujah!"

Christianity was introduced into Scotland, according to Bede, by St. Ninian, a British bishop, A.D. 412. Shortly afterwards the heathenism of Ireland was swept away, and Christianity established as the national religion, through the labours of St. Patrick. The birth-place of this famous Saint has been identified as Kirkpatrick, near Glasgow. His father was a deacon and his grandfather a priest. His original name was Succat, which means "strong in war." His Roman name was Patricius—whence Patrick. He was captured in his youth by Irish pirates and sold as a slave. While herding cattle, drenched with rain and numbed with cold, he felt himself summoned by a Divine voice to make known the true God to his captors and their countrymen. Obedient to the heavenly vision, he escaped to France, and sought training in the monastic school of Tours for his life work.

Returning to his adopted country with a company of fellow labourers in missionary toil, he preached everywhere, as he had opportunity, the Gospel of Jesus. He came one Eastertide to the famous hill of Tara, the ancient residence of the

Irish kings. It was a high festival of the Druids and the bards, when no fire might be lighted under pain of death. Nevertheless the intrepid missionary calmly pitched his tent and kindled his camp fire. As the smoke curled upwards in the still air of the Easter eve, it was seen by the Druids, and caused the greatest consternation. The act of the missionary was regarded as one of sacriligious enormity, and the Druids warned the king that unless it were extinguished forthwith, to him whose fire it was would belong the sovereignty of Ireland for ever. The Saint was summoned to the presence of the king. With great boldness and eloquence he preached the Gospel to the assembled Druids. So successful were his labours that many chiefs were baptized, and soon the great idol of Crom-cruach, in the plain of Magh Slecht, in what is now the County of Cavan, was destroyed.

A prominent feature of the pagan worship of Ireland at that time was the adoration of the sun. St. Patrick proclaimed a mightier Deity— One who made the sun, but who was Himself uncreated and eternal. "Beside Him," he said, "there is no other God, nor ever was, nor shall be." "Those who believe in Him," he declared, "would rise again in the glory of the true Sun, that is, the glory of Jesus Christ, being by redemption sons of God and joint heirs of the Christ, of whom, and by whom, and to whom are all things; for the true Sun, Jesus Christ, shall never wane or set, nor shall any perish who do His will, but they shall live forever, even as He liveth forever with God the Father Almighty and the Holy Spirit, world without end."*

With such sublime teachings the Saint confronted the paganism of Ireland, and, like the mists of darkness before the dawn of day, it faded away before the growing light of the Sun of Righteousness. With the characteristic enthusiasm of the Celtic race, the impulsive Irish opened their hearts to the reception of the truth, and welcomed as a teacher sent from God the messenger of the new evangel. He was not, however, without stern opposition and bitter persecution from the pagans, and many were his "hair-breadth 'scapes," and, if we would believe the traditions, his miraculous deliverances.

With a wise foresight, the Saint devoted himself especially to the establishment of schools and seminaries for the training of a native clergy for the conversion of Ireland. As years passed on he made his principal abode at Armagh, where gathered about him those ecclesiastical institutions which made that ancient city the religious

* "Confession" of Saint Patrick.

metropolis of the island. Here he spent the last years of his life. Here he wrote the "Confession," from which the facts of this history are taken. He never revisited his own kindred in Scotland, though often solicited and urged thereto. A deep concern for his adopted country, and a sense of responsibility for its welfare, prevented his leaving it even for a time.

For seventy years he laboured with his disciples among his adopted people. They covered the island with churches and schools, where the Scriptures were studied, ancient books collected, and missionaries trained for duty, who, for hundreds of years thereafter, successfully proclaimed the Gospel, not only in their own country, but also throughout the remotest parts of Europe. The doctrines of St. Patrick were not those of pure Protestantism, but they were unstained with the corruptions into which Romanism subsequently degenerated. His labours conferred inestimable blessings, not only upon Ireland, but upon almost every nation of Continental Europe.

"The legends of the 'Isle of Saints,'" says Kingsley, "are full of Irish poetry and tenderness, and not without touches of genuine Irish humour. The memory of the virtues and beneficence of the Saints, as well as of their miracles, is rooted in the heart and brain of the Irish peasantry, and has been an enduring heirloom of the Irish race through long, sad centuries of oppression and misrule."

Ireland soon repaid to Scotland her debt of obligation. Among the wild mountains of Donegal, early in the sixth century, was born a child destined to become famous throughout the world as the Apostle of Christianity among the heathen Picts, and the Patron Saint of Scotland, till he was superseded by St. Andrew. The boy received at baptism the name of *Colum*, to which was afterwards added *cille*, or "of the Church," on account of his devout attendance on the ordinances of religion. Eventually it was changed to Columba,—*i.e.*, the Dove,—under which name he was canonized.

The youth had a passion for borrowing and copying manuscripts of the Gospels and Psalms. By stealth, we read, he copied in the Church of Drom Finn, in Ulster, remaining after service for that purpose, a Psalter belonging to Finnian, the priest, which he despaired of getting otherwise. The priest discovered the pious fraud, but kept his own counsel till the slow and tiresome labour was accomplished. He then demanded the book because it had been copied without his permission from one which was his property. Columba refused to comply, and appealed to Diarmaid, King of Ireland, for his decision. The case was argued before the king, in the royal palace of Tara. Diarmaid gave the following judgment, which passed into a proverb, which is current in Ireland to this day: *Le gach boin a boinin, le gach leabhar a leabhran*—that is, "To every cow belongeth her little cow or calf," and so to every book belongeth its son-book or copy: "therefore the book you wrote, O Colum, belongs of right to Finnian."

The indignant Colum denounced the injustice of this judgment and fled to his native mountains of Donegal. Here he raised a party of his kinsmen who, after the manner of their race, enthusiastically took up his quarrel. Forming an alliance with the King of Connaught, they marched against Diarmaid. A bloody battle was fought at Cooldrevny, in Sligo, in which many were slain. Compunction of conscience now visited the blood-guilty Columba, who had been so unlike the dove which his name signified. He was condemned by the Church to quit his own country, and win to Christ from among the heathen as many souls as had perished in battle. So runs the ancient legend, in testimony of which is preserved, in the museum of the Royal Irish Academy, the *Cathach* or "Book of Battle," which is alleged to be the identical MS. Psalter which had been the cause of this strange conflict. As a potent relic of the Saint, it was borne into battle as late as 1497, to ensure the victory of the O'Donnell clan.

Faithfully did Columbia fulfil his expiatory vow.

With twelve companions, in skin-covered osier boats, he reached Iona's lonely isle, amid the stormy Hebrides. Here he reared his monastery of wattled huts, his chapel, refectory, cow byres, and grange. The bare ground was their bed and a stone their pillow. The sea-girt isle became a distinguished seat of learning and piety—a moral lighthouse, sending forth rays of spiritual illumination amid the dense heathen darkness all around. Much time was spent by the monks in the study of the Greek and Latin tongues, and in the transcription of MS. copies of the Scriptures, many of which, still extant, are wonderful examples of the art of copying and illuminating.

The pious Culdees, as these missionaries were called, in their fragile osier barks, penetrated the numerous gulfs and straits of that storm-lashed coast. The carried the Gospel to the far-off steeps of St. Kilda; to the Orkney, Shetland, and Faroe islands; and even to Iceland itself, where relics of their visit, in Celtic books, bells, and crosses, have been found. Three hundred monasteries and churches are ascribed to their pious toil, some of which survived the stormy tumults of a thousand years.

Other Irish and British monks carried the Gospel to remote Bergundian plains, to Swiss valleys and German forests, and even far-off Sclavic wildernesses. With coarse serge dress and pastoral staff, with leathern water-bottle, a wallet, a leathern case for their service books and another for the relics of some Saint or martyr, they went forth to conquer the world for Christ. These monks became the apostles and civilizers of Europe.

With the decrepitude, decay, and breaking up of the old Roman Empire, the very foundations of society seemed dissolved, and Europe reverted to a condition of barbarism. Crushed by a merciless weight of taxation, and drained of their strength by the levies of the Imperial armies, the older provinces almost ceased to till the soil. The villages disappeared out of the land, the towns crumbled to ruin, and dense forests of oak, birch, aspen, and witch elm overspread once fair and populous regions, and enveloped Central Europe in a vast network of silence and shade.* Wave after wave of northern invasion—Celt, Teuton, Sclave, and Hun—swept over the scene, burying

---

* Montalambert—"Monks of the West."

beneath ruin and destruction the remains of classic civilization.

The Christian Church was almost the only institution that survived the wreck of the old Roman world. Throughout the long, dark, stormy night of the middle ages it trimmed the lamp of learning, which else had flickered to extinction. With no small admixture of error, it nourished the germs of undying good. It asserted the dignity of humanity, rebuked the tyranny of nobles and of kings, smote the yoke from the neck of the slave, maintained the sanctity of human life, and, in an age of violence and blood, exhibited the immeasurable superiority of moral influence to brute force. The monks were the Apostles and the Saints of medieval Europe. St. Guthlac in Lincoln's fens and on Yorkshire wolds; St. Columba in lone Iona and on storm-swept Lindisfarne; St. Boniface amid Thuringian forests; St. Columbanus in Helvetian vales; Methodius and Cyril amid the recesses of Bohemia and Bulgaria; and Anskar amid Norwegian glaciers and fjords raised the voice of prayer and hymn of praise, and planted the germs of the new life of Christendom.

Another paper will trace the reconversion of England under Augustine.

We now return to trace more particularly the history of Christianity in Britain:

When Hengist and Horsa with their wild pagan followers, in the middle of the fifth century, invaded England, they found most of the inhabitants of the south and a smaller proportion in the north, at least nominal Christians. The storm of Saxon invasion burst with equal violence on tower and temple. "Amidst the havoc of an exterminating warfare," says a judicious authority, "the churches were destroyed and the ecclesiastics massacred, so that at length the former Christianity of the country was chiefly to be traced by heaps of ashes and tokens of devastation." Without a clergy, without altars or churches, and without the rites of religion, Christianity became almost extinct. But in the providence of God a course of events, seemingly trivial in character, was bringing about its re-establishment. The story is a familiar one, but it will bear repetition.

About the year A.D. 577, a monk of the monastery of St. Andrew at Rome was one day passing through the market place. He saw there, among the gang of slaves exposed for sale, three fair-skinned, blue-eyed, flaxen-haired boys. Their ruddy beauty excited his interest, and he asked the slave dealer of what country they were.

"They are Angles, father," was the reply.

"Not Angles but angels would they be if they were Christians," he exclaimed.

"From what province do they come?" he further inquired.

"From Deira,* father," the slave dealer answered.

"*De ira Dei liberandi sunt,*" continued the monk, playing upon the name, "from the wrath of God they are to be delivered. And who is the king of this province," he continued.

"Æla," was the reply.

"Allelujah," exclaimed the pious monk, as if inspired with the spirit of prophecy, "the praise of God yet shall be chanted in that clime."

His heart yearned for the conversion of that fair pagan race, and he soon after set forth as a missionary to tell them of the glorious tidings of the Gospel. He was recalled, however, by the ruling pope, and his generous purpose was for the time postponed. A few years later that monk became Gregory the Great, Pope of Rome. His long-cherished object was now about to be fulfilled. He selected a band of forty monks and sent them forth with their prior Augustine to plant again the religion of the Cross on the soil of Britain.

In the summer of the year 596, they set forth

* The region now included in Yorkshire and Durham.

on their momentous mission. They traversed rapidly the plains of Lombardy, crossed the Gallic Alps, and reached the town of Aix in Provence. But the timorous monks were so dismayed by the accounts they received of the ferocity of the Saxons that they refused to proceed and sent to Gregory for permission to return. The zealous pontiff, however, adjured them by every Christian motive to persevere in their sacred task, and he wrote letters on their behalf to the kings and bishops of the Franks. Constrained by an authority they dared not resist, the missionary band advanced through Tours and Anjou to the sea coast. They took ship the following spring and soon reached the Isle of Thanet on the coast of Kent.

The time and place were propitious for the success of their mission. Ethelbert, the King of Kent, held the important rank of Bretwalda, or chief king of the Heptarchy. Moreover, his queen, Bertha, was a Frankish princess, brought up, at least nominally, in the Christian faith. Ethelbert was therefore, although a pagan, probably predisposed to a favourable reception of the new doctrines. Indeed, tradition records that he was not without previous admonition of the supernatural claims of the religion of Christ, possibly from Frankish palmers who had wandered into his kingdom. Alexander Smith, in his beautiful poem "Edwin of Deira," has interwoven the various traditions of the conversion of Britain, though sometimes with slight anachronism, into consecutive narrative. I shall quote largely from the poem the account of this important event, of such intense interest to the whole English-speaking race. To the king's palace is represented as having come, months before the advent of Augustine,

"—— A poor far-travelled man who spoke
About a dear God Christ, who hung on tree
While His own children pierced His tender side.
Quoth he, 'This English land belongs to Christ,
And all the souls upon it. He will come,
And merciful possession take of all.' . . . .
"Then said he, 'When Lord Christ
Comes to His own, then the times of war are o'er.
Upon His raiment there are stains of blood.
But 'tis His own, for He can only love.
He never blew a trumpet in the field;
His soldiers are the men who die in fires,
With blessings on their lips for those who stack
The fagots and who bring the blazing torch.'"

When tidings was brought to the king, whom the poet by a solecism calls Edwin, of the landing of Augustine's vessel, he rode down with his lords to witness the debarkation of this strange embassy.

"In the bright
Fringe of the living sea a great ship lay,

And o'er the sands a grave procession paced
Melodious with many a chaunting voice.
Nor spear nor buckler had these foreign men;
Each wore a snowy robe that downward flowed;
Fair in their front a silver cross they bore;
A painted Saviour floated in the wind;
The chaunting voices, as they rose and fell,
Hallowed the rude sea air. All the lords
Sat silent and wide-eyed. The foremost man,
Who seemed the leader of the white-robed train,
Unbent, although his beard was white as snow,
And the veins branched along his withered hands,
Spake, while to Edwin he obeisance made.
' To thee, who bear'st the likeness of a king,
'Tis fit that I should speak, that thou may'st know
What is the business of thy servants here.
We come to traffic not in horse or man,
Corn, wine, or oil; nor yet to gather gold,
Nor to win cities by the force of arms.
O king! we came across the dangerous seas
To win thee and thy people from the gods
Who cannot hear a cry or answer prayer,
Unto the worship of the heavenly Christ,
Of whom thou art the eldest son of all
That in this nation dwell. Within thy hands
Thou hast our lives. But yet we trust in Christ,
From whose pure hand each king derives his crown,
And in whose keeping are the heavenly worlds,
No harm shall us befall. We bring thee Christ—
The Christ before whose coming devils flee,
Idolatrous fires burn low, and horrid drums,
Beaten to drown the shrieks of sacrifice,
Are covered o'er with silence.' "

The king received them courteously and appointed a time for a formal interview, but with characteristic caution he declined to receive them under a roof, for fear of the charms or spells which he imagined they might exercise upon him.

"'To-morrow, here, beneath the open sky,
Where magical arts are powerless, will I bring
In council all my lords, and ancient men
Who have inherited wisdom with their snows,
To give thee patient hearing. For myself,
Although not minded to desert the gods
My fathers followed, and beneath whose sway
The happy seasons still have come and gone,
I keep an open door for thoughts and men
That wear strange clothes and speak with foreign tongues;
Such hospitality befits a king.'
And when the priests, the cross before them borne,
Beheld the city in the yellow light,
And all the king's train riding to the gate,
Sudden a choir of silver voices rose:—
'Lord Christ, we do beseech Thee in Thy grace,
Let not Thine anger 'gainst this city burn,
Nor 'gainst Thy holy house, for we have sinned!'
And so they sang until the gate was reached."

The king was sorely puzzled in his mind. He was reluctant to abandon the old gods under whom he had achieved victory and become great. At the same time there was a strange power in the words of those foreign teachers that took hold upon his conscience and swayed his soul, he knew not why. And thus he reasoned with himself—

"'This Christ has ne'er been seen by living eye,
His voice has ne'er been heard by living ear,
And if beneath His banner I enlist,
Service life-long, obedience absolute,
Strict abstinence from all ambitious thoughts,
Stern curbing of the war-horse in the heart,
Are needed; and long years of purity,
That shame the honour of a knight, that shame
The nobleness of kings. War is forbid;
I must forgive the man that injures me.
What if, when I am on a death-bed laid,
Hoary with painful years, no Christ should be?
I have my spirit tortured for a dream;
The man who wrongs me insolently laughs;
And unenlarged my kingdom for my son;
And, unembalmed by victories, my name
Will perish like a nothing from the earth,
Unrescued by a harpstring. Could I place
This Christ within the temple of the gods?
One must be right! But then this man brings Christ
To save me from the worship of the gods,
To smite in dust their shrines.'"

As he thus questioned with himself in the hush and silence of the night a supernatural presence visited him,—so runs the poem,—and drew aside the veil that hides the future from men's view. And thus it spoke—

"'This fertile island in the narrow seas,
Parcelled in seven states that fret and fume
Fiercely against each other, shall grow one,
And a far distant son of thine shall sit
Within its capital city high enthroned,
The crown upon his head. The crown from Christ

> He will receive on coronation day.
> The kingdoms and the nations of the earth
> Are tools with which Christ works; and many He
> Hath broken, for the metal faithless proved;
> And many He hath thrown aside to rust
> In a neglected corner; many worn
> With noble service into nothingness;
> This England, when 'tis tempered to His need,
> Will be His instrument to shape the world
> For many a thousand years. O mighty Prince,
> Within the East is born a day of days,
> For Christ this day will to thy kingdom come
> And seek therein to dwell. Be faithful thou,
> That faithfulness may live from king to king.'

The king holds council with the priests and wise men of his realm. Some endeavour to dissuade him from acknowledging the foreign gods. At length rose Ella, a venerable priest, hoary with a hundred years, and said—

> "'To me, O king, this present life of man
> Seems, in comparison of unknown time,
> Like a swift sparrow flying through a room,
> Wherein thou sitt'st at supper with thy lords,
> A good fire in the midst, while out of doors
> In gusty darkness whirls the furious snow
> That wall and window blocks. The sparrow flies
> In at one door, and by another out,
> Brief space of warm and comfortable air
> It knows in passing, then it vanishes
> Into the gusty dark from whence it came.
> The soul like that same sparrow comes and goes,
> This life is but a moment's sparrow-flight
> Between the two unknowns of birth and death;

> An arrow's passage from an unknown bow
> Toward an unknown bourne. O king, I have
> This matter meditated all my days,
> And questioned death, but with no more effect
> Than if I shouted 'gainst a stormy wind
> And had my words dashed back in my own face.
> If therefore these new doctrines bring me light,
> All things I would renounce to follow them.'"

The eventful day, fraught with the destinies of England, at length arrived. The band of missionaries, after much prayer to God, issued from the house in which they lodged, in solemn procession, clad in snowy vestments, chanting holy litanies, bearing on high a silver cross and the painted image of the Saviour. It was an age of sign and symbol, and to these they largely trusted to impress the infantile imagination of that untaught race. As they reached the place of conclave, the leader of the missionary band stood forth and thus addressed the multitude—

> "'Fair island people, blue-eyed, golden-haired,
> That dwell within a green delicious land
> With noble cities as with jewels set—
> A land all shadowed by full-acorned woods,
> Refreshed and beautified by stately streams—
> We heard this island with its climate pure
> Was given o'er to heathen deities:
> That these were worshipped with the bended knee
> Unholy fire, and smoke of sacrifice.
> And we are come to smite the deities,
> And to the idolatrous temples set the torch.

For this we took our lives within our hands,
For this we drew a furrow through the sea,
And this we will accomplish ere we die.
And furthermore, we come to speak of Christ,
Who from His heaven looked down, and saw a world
Crimson with stains of wicked battle-fields,
And loud with the oppressions of the poor,
And, moved with gracious pity, wrapt the sun
Of His Divinity in a mortal cloud
Till it was tempered to our human sight.
And, for the love He bore the race of men,
Full thirty years ungrudgingly He breathed
Our human breath, endured our human needs,
Hungered and thirsted, oft without a home.
Though but a man He seemed, such virtue dwelt
Within the compass of His mortal frame,
That poor and forlorn creatures near their death
Touched by His garments were made instant whole.
And all the time He lived upon the earth
He cast out devils, gave the blind their sight;
With slender store of loaves and fishes fed
A hungry multitude close-ranged on grass;
And, walking on the waters, with a word
Made all the roaring lake of Galilee
Sink to a glassy mirror for the stars.
Yea, at His word a three days' buried man
Came forth to light with grave-clothes on his face
And, when the times of wickedness were full,
When by the vilest city in the world
Nailed to a cross upreared against the sky
He hung with malefactors—dismal sight
The sun dared not to look on—with a prayer
For him who pierced His body with the spear,
For him who tore His temples with the thorns,
For him who mocked His thirst with vinegar,

The Lord Christ bleeding bowed His head and died·
And by that dying did He wash earth white
From murders, battles, lies, ill deeds, and took
Remorse away that feeds upon the heart
Like slow fire on a brand. From grave He **burst**
Death could not hold Him, and **ere many days**
Before the **eyes of those that did Him love**
He **passed up through yon ocean of** blue air
Unto the heaven of heavens, whence He came.
And there He sits this moment, man and God;
Strong as a God, flesh-hearted as a man,
And all the uncreated light confronts
With eyelids that have known the touch of tears.
Marvel not, king, that we have come to thee.
If but one man stood on the farthest shore,
Thither I would adventure with the news—
News that undungeons all from sin and fear.
The glimmering wisp, the sprite that haunts the ford,
The silent ghost that issues from the grave
Like a pale smoke that takes the **dead man's form**
Can scare us never more, for Christ made **all,**
And lays His ear so close unto the world
That in lone desert, peril, or thick night,
A whispered prayer can reach it. In the still
Abyss of midnight **lives a human heart,**
And therefore all the loneliness and space,
And all the icy splendours, cannot freeze.
Death is a dinted couch; for there a space.
Christ's limbs have rested, and that knowledge takes
The loneliness, which is death's fear, away.
And in the light beyond earth's shade **He sits**
With all the happy **spirits of the dead**
Silent as garden flowers that **feed on air,**
And thither thou wilt join **Him** in due time.
          " 'Chr:st **cannot come**
Where any idol is; so burn them down.

King, be the wind to blow these clouds away,
That Christ's clear sky may overarch thy land.'"

Whereupon Coifi, the high-priest of the false gods, giant-moulded, strong of limb, impetuous of soul, in an outburst of enthusiasm born of the intense convictions of his mind, exclaimed—

"'O King, give ear unto the stranger's words,
Surely the truest, best that ever ear
Gave welcome habitation to. The deities
Are but the mighty shadows of ourselves,
And reach no higher than our highest moods.
But this Christ has existence all untouched
By fond imagination or belief:
And, being Lord, the richly furnished world
Is an unemptied treasury of gifts
For those He loves; and, on rebellious men,
He has for executioners the sea,
Snow-drift, and sun-fire, blast, and thunderstone,
Earthquake and shivering lightnings red with haste:
All good is resident within His smile,
All terror in His frown. And, therefore, King,
It seems to me expedient that the gods,
Voiceless and empty-handed as our dreams
Should be at once forsaken, and the torch
Be set unto the temples we have built.'"

The wavering mind of the king was swayed toward the truth. He resolved to embrace this strange new doctrine of the Cross, and to take allegiance as the crowned servant of the lowly Man of Nazareth. And thus, in kingly wise, he spoke—

"'Ye strangers who have come across the sea,
Ye people who have known me all my days,
I here, in seeing of the earth and sky,
Unclothe myself of the religion dark
Which I and all my forefathers have worn,
And put on Christ, like raiment white and clean.
Ye priests, I take allegiance unto Christ;
My crown I wear as vassal unto Him:
This day I Christ as my commander take,
And as His faithful soldier will I live,
And as His faithful soldier will I die.
But, being now His soldier, it is meet
That I make war upon His enemies;
Who of my priests and nobles standing round
Will first profane the temples of the gods
And all the dark enclosures sacred held?'"

The impetuous high-priest, with the characteristic enthusiasm of a new convert, sprang eagerly forward and exclaimed—

"'I will, O King;
For surely of thy people it befits
No one so well as him who was their priest.
If I the dwellings of the gods outrage,
With a forbidden horse, unlawful spear,
And smite them and return again unhurt,
What then? Yon ancient boulder on the hill
That wears obscure the features of a man,
Is strong, divine, and worshipful as they.
But, if the blow and clangour of my lance
Should pierce the stony calm, and draw a voice
And lightnings that will blast me, I but die,
And by my death I bring the gods alive,
And in the fairer summers that will come

My name will be remembered oft with praise.
The profanation of the gods is mine ;
Provide me, **King**, a stallion and a spear.' "

Dire was the confusion that thereupon ensued. The multitude stood in awe-struck suspense, awaiting the result of this sacrilegious act. It was like the conflict betwixt Elijah and the priests of Baal. The worshippers of the false gods eagerly expected their outraged deities to avenge their insult on their recreant priest.

"Soon from the tumult running footmen broke
Leading the coal-black stallion of the king
That plunged and neighed, his knee and counter dashed
With foamy flakes, and on him Coifi sprang,
Priest-vested as he was, and curbed and reined
The mighty brute as though his heels were armed,
And loud cuirass and greave his daily wear.
While with his hoofs the stallion bruised the turf,
Coifi leaned sideways, stretched a hand and caught
A glittering spear, and, poising it, gave rein
And rode toward the temple, and the crowd,
Deeming the priest stark mad or brain-distract,
In that he was so covetous of death,
Broke after him in wild and shrieking lines ;
But Coifi struck them marble as he crashed
Through the enclosures ever sacred held,
And gained the central space unharmed, and rode
Thrice round and round, then in his stirrup stood,
And, with a high defiance on his lip,
Smote, with a clang, an idol, monster-faced ;
And, as he smote, the foul thing, reeling, fell ;
Fell Dagon-like, face downwards on the grass.

And, when from every heart the icy hand
Of fear was lifted, sea-like grew the noise.
And Coifi shouted something from the place,
And, as in answer to the half-heard shout,
The king's loud voice the mighty uproar clove,
'Consume with fire the idols and their homes;
Burn stake and god together!' And the cries
Within the crowds a sacred fury wrought,
The deities were tumbled on the grass,
The pales and the enclosures were torn down
By naked hands, and flung into a heap,
And one a torch applied; and through the smoke
There flickered here and there the fiery tongues
That crackled, spread, and ever higher climbed;
Till the scorched beam came thundering down, and towers
Of flame rushed up, then licked the air and died.
And when the world was quivering through a film
Of furnace heat that shook in welling lines,
And a great smoke rolled off and sea-ward spread,
And dimmed the gleam from headland on to cape,
And ever louder grew the swarming crowds
The white-robed priests together standing sang,
'Down falls the wicked idol on his face,
So let all wicked gods and idols fall!
Come forth, O light, from out the breaking East,
And with thy splendour pierce the heathen dark,
And morning make on continent and isle
That thou may'st reap the harvest of thy tears,
O Holy One that hung upon the tree.'

"So, when the temple lay a ruined mass,
And the gorged flames were low upon the brand,
And a great vapour breathed across the sea,
King Edwin called his people; and they came
Long line on line as tide sets to the shore.
And then he pointed to the smoky blot

Athwart the sea-light and the peaceful sky.
'Behold our old religion hanging there,
Behold it dying in the heavenly ray;
So dies the error of a thousand years!'"

Then, in the great gladness of their hearts, the choir of white-robed priests fulfilled the prophecy of Gregory, made years before in the market place of Rome, by chanting "Allelujah" to the Lord for the bloodless victory His hand had wrought. They joyously exclaimed—

"'The holy Pontiff's heart,
That aches with the great darkness of the world,
Is this day lightened, for among the tongues
That rise to heaven in prayer, there is one
Ne'er heard by Christ before; another string
Is to the world-harp added, praising Christ.
For what has been accomplished on this day
Fragrant will Gregory's memory be held
By every race of Englishmen to be.'"

A nation was born in a day. The king, with several of the great lords of his court, was baptized on Whitsuntide, the feast of Pentecost, June 2nd, A.D. 597. The conversion of the sovereign was the signal, as was frequently the case in those loyal days, for that of the people; and on the following Christmas day upwards of ten thousand were baptized in the waters of the Swale at the mouth of the Medway. After his conversion Ethelbert became exceedingly zealous in the extension of the kingdom of Christ and in subduing all England to His sway.

"And from that day, filled with strange fire, he rode
A mighty idol-breaker, far and wide
In battle-gear, Christ following in the print
Of his war-horses hoofs. The fanes he burned
At Goodmanham, at Yeverin, and York,
And Cateret where the Swale runs shallowing by
Near his own city, where the temple stood,
He raised to Christ a simple church of stone,
And ruled his people faithfully, until he died.
        " And so they laid
Within the church of stone, with many a tear,
The body of the earliest Christian king
That England knew; there 'neath the floor he sleeps,
With lord and priest around, till through the air
The angel of the resurrection flies."

ST. BONIFACE, THE APOSTLE OF GERMANY.

No records of missionary adventure exhibit nobler heroism than those relating the story of the introduction of Christianity into the Pagan wilderness of Central Europe. Its rude superstitions gave place reluctantly to the gentler genius of the Gospel. The stern mythology of the north seemed to find somewhat akin in the rugged strength of the Teutonic races. But the religion of the cross was shown to be no less adapted to the rudest and most barbaric natures than to those of the highest culture and refinement.

All Protestant Christendom is indebted to a German monk for emancipating the souls of men from the spiritual thraldom of Rome. It was to an English monk that, eight hundred years before, the German lands were indebted for the first preaching of the Gospel, not yet corrupted with the papal superstitions by which it became subsequently degraded.

Near the ancient city of Exeter, in the beautiful county of Devon, was born, towards the close of the seventh century, Winfrid, the future apostle of Germany. He was carefully educated in a conventual school, the only sanctuary of learning in those stormy days. He was designed by his parents for secular life, but a dangerous illness turned his thoughts towards serious things. He became eminent for his diligence and devotion, and for his deep acquaintance with the Scriptures. In his thirtieth year he received ordination, and his remarkable eloquence and superior talents and learning won for him great repute as a preacher. He was honoured with the confidence of King Ina, of Wessex, and the way to fame and fortune seemed open for him in his native land.

But a nobler ambition fired his soul. A few years before Willibrord, a Northumbrian monk, educated in one of those Irish monasteries which were then the most famous for learning and piety in Europe, had gone with twelve companions as a missionary to Frisia, as the low fen lands of Belgium and Holland were then called. They met with great success and great persecution; and some of them won the coveted crown of martyrdom. The tales of their heroic deeds stirred the heart of the English monk and he burned to emulate the zeal, and to share the trial and triumph and the everlasting reward of his countrymen who were toiling among the pagan Frisians. He was destined to surpass them all in suffering and success and in perennial fame wherever the records of Christian heroism are remembered.

In the year 717, he sailed from London, even then a busy port, to the coast of Normandy. Joining a band of pilgrims he proceeded on foot through France and over the Gallic Alps to Rome. From Pope Gregory II. he obtained a commission to preach the Gospel among the pagan tribes of Germany. In the following spring, therefore, with a band of fellow missionaries he traversed the plains of Lombardy, climbed the rugged Swiss Alps, threaded the wilds of the Black Forest, full of elk and bison, bear and wolf, lynx and glutton and, for all he knew, of worst beasts still. Arrived in the heart of ancient Thuringia, he opened his commission. The wild German ritters were not impervious to the truth. Their stern hearts melted at the tender story of Calvary and converts were made to the religion of Jesus.

Rejecting an invitation to become bishop of Utrecht in the Frisian land, which had become partially Christianized, Boniface plunged into the wilds of Hesse. Multitudes of the fierce Saxons, subdued by the power of the Cross, soon received baptism at his hands. Nevertheless his converts were prone to relapse into paganism or, in strange confusion, to blend their old superstitions with their new creed. At Geismar, in Hesse, stood an ancient oak sacred for ages to Thor, the god of thunder. It was the object of peculiar reverence and was the rendezvous of the heathen assemblies of the neighbouring tribes. In vain Boniface argued and entreated against its idolatrous veneration. He therefore boldly resolved to destroy the idol, for such in reality it was. He advanced, axe in hand, to cut down the obnoxious giant of the forest. A vast multitude assembled, restrained from interference by a sense of awe and terror. Many expected the instant destruction of the intrepid monk by the power of the outraged deity. But blow fell on blow and still Thor gave no sign. In vain his votaries invoked his power. Like Baal he was on a journey or was sleeping and heeded not their prayers. At length the mighty monarch of the woods shivered through all his leafy branches, tottered on his throne, reeled crashing down and lay prone upon the ground, shattered into pieces by the fall. The vast multitude were convinced that the Lord, He is the God, and from the timber of their fallen idol was constructed an oratory for the worship of Christ.

Soon throughout the Schwartzwald, writes the historian of the conversion of Germany, "the heathen temples disappeared; humble churches rose amid the forest glades; monastic buildings sprang up wherever salubrity of soil and the presence of running water suggested an inviting site; the land was cleared and brought under the plough; and the sound of prayer and praise awoke unwonted echoes in the forest aisles. The harvest truly was plenteous but the labourers were few."

Boniface therefore sent an urgent appeal for assistance to his native land. He addressed a circular letter, A.D. 733, to the bishops, clergy, and principal abbots of England, in which he says: "We beseech you, that ye will remember us in your prayers to God and our Lord Jesus Christ, who would have all men be saved and come to a knowledge of the truth, that He will vouchsafe to convert to the true faith the hearts of the heathen Saxons, that they may be delivered from the snares of the Evil One, wherewith they are now held captive. Have compassion on them, brethren. They often say, 'We are of one blood with our brothers in England.' Remember they are your kinsmen according to the flesh. Remember that the time for working is short, for the end of all things is at hand, and death cannot praise God, nor can any give Him thanks in the grave. Aid us then while it is day."

He especially besought the donation of copies of different portions of Holy Scripture. Of the Abbess of Eadburgh he requested the epistles of St. Peter, written in gilt letters, that he might use them in preaching. From another he asked copies of the Gospels written in clear, bold hand, suitable to the weakness of his eyes. He requested also the commentaries of the venerable Bede for the elucidation of the sacred text.

These truly apostolic appeals were not in vain. Zealous missionary recruits flocked from England, among whom were not a few devout women who braved the perils of a stormy sea and the greater perils of a journey through roadless forests, in order to become deaconesses and servants of the Church in the wilderness. The wild, heathen German land of lawless ritters, bandits, and robbers was being organized into a Christian community. Churches were multiplied and the bishoprics of Wurzburg, Eichstadt, Bamberg, Erfurt, Mayence, Worms, Spires, Tongres, Fulda, Salzburg, Passau, Cologne, and Utrecht, destined to become during later centuries great historic cities of manifold associations both of glory and of shame, were founded.

The venerable missionary—venerable both by his years and his apostolic character— boldly rebuked sin in high places. The smiles or frowns of earthly potentates inspired in him neither hope nor fear. Learning that King Ethelbald of England was living a life of flagrant sin, he administered a scathing reproof and tried to shame him into repentance by contrasting his conduct with that of the pagan Saxons in the German forests, who, though without the law of Christianity, did by nature the things contained in the law, and testified by stern punishments their abhorrence of the crimes committed by the recreant Christian king.

Though bowed beneath the weight of years and labours manifold, the missionary ardour of this apostolic bishop knew no abatement. Six times he crossed the Alps in the interest of his vast mission field. The welfare of his spiritual flock was a burden that lay heavy on his heart. In his seventy-fifth year he was called upon to restore upwards of thirty churches which had been destroyed by inroads of the heathen Frisians. He made an urgent appeal to Pepin of France for the protection of the persecuted Church. "Nearly all my companions," he wrote, "are strangers in this land. Some are aged men who have long borne, with me, the burden and heat of the day. For all these I am full of anxiety, lest after my death they should be scattered as sheep having no shepherd. Let them have a share of your countenance and protection, that they may not be dispersed abroad, and that the people dwelling on the heathen borders may not lose the law of Christ. My clergy are in deep poverty. Bread they can obtain, but clothing they cannot procure unless they receive aid to enable them to persevere and endure their hardships. Let me know whether thou canst promise the granting of my request, that, whether I live or die, I may have some assurance for the future."

This truly apostolic epistle brings to us across the dim and stormy centuries the assurance of the faith and prayers and godly zeal with which the foundations of the Christian civilization of the German Vaterland were laid by this pious English monk so many hundred years ago.

His work was well-nigh done. His death was as heroic as his life. Though upwards of seventy-five years of age, his missionary zeal burned as brightly as when in his eager youth in his English home he yearned to preach the Gospel to the pagan tribes. He resolved to make a dying effort to win the heathen Frisians to the religion of Jesus. He had already selected his successor in office, and he bade him a solemn farewell. Among the books which he took as his companions on his last journey was the treatise of St. Ambrose on "The Advantage of Death," with which he sustained his soul as he went calmly to his fate. He felt an assurance that he should not return, and directed that with his travelling equipment his shroud might also be put up.

With a retinue of ten ecclesiastics and forty laymen he embarked at Mayence, on the Rhine, on his last missionary expedition. He glided down the rapid river, whose castled crags are haunted still with old time memories. At length they reached the dreary fen land of the heathen Frisians. For a time all went well. Many pagans were converted and several churches were planted. But the heathen party, enraged at the success of the missionary band, resolved on an exterminating blow. On a blithe June morning the shimmer of spear points was seen approaching the Christian encampment. Soon the clash of arms and shouts of an infuriate multitude were heard. Some of the Bishop's retinue counselled resistance and began to prepare for a defence. But the venerable Boniface stepped forth from his tent, his white hair streaming in the wind, and gave command that not a weapon should be lifted, but that all should calmly await the crown of martyrdom.

"Let us not return evil for evil," said the dying Saint. "The long-expected day has come. The time of our departure is at hand. Strengthen ye yourselves in the Lord, and He will redeem your souls. Be not afraid of those who can only kill the body. Put all your trust in God who will speedily give you an entrance into His heavenly kingdom and an everlasting reward."

Enbraved by these heroic words, that doomed missionary band calmly awaited their fate. The onset of the heathen was furious. The struggle was brief, and soon the blood-bedabbled robes and gory ground and mutilated bodies were the mute witnesses of this dreadful tragedy. The victorious pagans eagerly ransacked the tents, but their only treasures were some leathern cases containing the precious parchment Gospels and other manuscripts of the monks. These were speedily rifled, and the books strewn upon the plain or hidden in the marsh. Pious hands afterwards gathered up with loving care these relics and conveyed them, with the body of the great missionary, to the monastery of Fulda which he had founded.

In a stone sarcophagus in the crypts of the monastery still sleep the remains of the Apostle of Germany, and here has been treasured for ages the time-worn copy of St. Ambrose on "The Advantage of Death," which, with his shroud, was stained with his blood. This simple relic brings vividly before the imagination that heroic martyrdom eleven hundred years ago—June 5th, A.D. 755—by the shores of the Zuyder Zee:

> Many centuries have been numbered
> While in death the monk has slumbered,
>   'Neath the convent's sculptured portal,
>   Mingling with the common dust :

> But the brave deed through the ages,
> Living in historic pages,
>   Brighter grows and gleams immortal,
>   Unconsumed by **moth or** rust.

This heroic **life and death** are but one example of the pious zeal of the mediaeval apostles and missionaries of Europe. " Eager, ardent, impetuous," writes Dr. Maclear, "they seemed to take the continent by storm. With a dauntless zeal that nothing could check, an enthusiasm that nothing could stay, they flung themselves into the gloomiest solitudes of Switzerland and Belgium and Germany, and before long their wooden huts made way for the statelier buildings of Luxeuil and Fulda and St. Gall. With practised eye they sought out the proper site for their monastic home, saw that it occupied a central position with reference to the tribes among whom they proposed to labour, that it possessed a fertile soil, that it was near some friendly water-course. These points secured, the word was given, the trees were felled, the forest cleared, the monastery arose. Soon the voice of prayer and praise was heard in those gloomy solitudes, the thrilling chant and **plaintive** litany awoke unwonted echoes amid the **forest glades.** The **brethren** were never idle. While some educated children whom they had redeemed from death or torture, others copied manuscripts or toiled over illuminated missal or transcribed a Gospel; others cultivated the soil, guided the plough, planted the apple-tree and the vine, arranged the bee-hives, erected the water-mill, opened the mine, and thus presented to the eyes of men the kingdom of Christ as the kingdom of One who had redeemed the bodies no less than the souls of His creatures."

Sturmi, a successor of Boniface, founded the first monastery in the awful forest of Burchwald. Unattended he sailed up lonely rivers and traversed pathless wildernesses where the foot of man had never trod before. By day he protected himself against wild beasts by chanting hymns and prayers. At night he kindled a fire of fagots, signed himself with the sign of the cross, and committed his soul to the protection of God. Before long he had four thousand monks under his command, felling the forest, ploughing the glebe— planting, tilling, building, dyking and draining— turning the wilderness into a garden, the scene of pagan savagery into the seat of Christian civilization. They conquered the wild heathen tribes, not with carnal weapons, for the monks were men of peace, but by the mightier weapon of Christ's Gospel; and often their own martyr-blood became the prolific seed of the Church.

The Western monk never exhibited the delirious fanaticism which marked the Eastern confraternities. He was characterised, in the earlier and purer days of monachism, by submission to authority, by intense missionary zeal, and by industry of life. "Beware of idleness," wrote St. Benedict, "as the greatest enemy of the soul." *Qui laborat orat*, was the motto of his order. Under the inspiration of this principle, work, before degraded as the task of slaves and serfs, became ennobled and dignified as a service of duty.

The Latin confraternities were also less austere and ascetic than the Eastern Orders. They exhibited less of spiritual selfishness and clearer conceptions of Christian obligation. " I serve God that I may save my lost soul," exclaimed the Stylite and, fakirlike, cursed the world as a scene of baleful enchantment, and in his dying hours refused to look upon the face or regard the tears of the mother who bore him. The gentle heart of St. Francis Assisi, the flower of the Western monks, went forth in affection to all created things, and inculcated boundless beneficence as the essence of Christianity. In his " Song of the Creatures," he gives thanks for his brother the sun, his sister the moon, his mother the earth, for the water, the fire and even for his sister Death—" Laudato sia Dio mio Signore—messer le frate sole—per suor luna—per nostra madre terra—nostra morte corporale."

But the monastic system, however clear in the spring, became miry in the stream. It shared an inveterate taint from which sprang frightful corruptions invoking its destruction. The picturesque ruins of the abbeys and priories of a bygone age are the monument of an institution out of harmony with the spirit of modern civilization—an institution to be remembered with gratitude, it is true, for its providential mission in the past, but without regret for its removal when that work had been accomplished. In lands where it still exists it is an anachronism and an incubus—a belated ghost of midnight walking in the light of day.

THE CONVERSION
OF
SWEDEN AND NORWAY.

> "Cross against corslet,
> Love against hatred,
> Peace-cry for war-cry,
> Patience is powerful;
> He that o'ercometh
> Hath power o'er the nations
>
> "Stronger than steel
> Is the sword of the Spirit;
> Swifter than arrows
> The light of the truth is;
> Greater than anger
> Is love, and subdueth."—*Saga of King Olaf*

"Who is the first and eldest of the gods?" asks the Scandinavian Edda, and gives the answer: 'He is called Allfadir. He lives from all ages and rules all things great and small. He made heaven and earth and all that they contain. He made man, and gave him a soul that shall live and never perish, though the body turn to mould or burn to ashes. His is an infinite power, a boundless knowledge, an incorruptible justice. He cannot be confined within the enclosure of walls, nor represented by any likeness of living thing."

Such was the sublime conception of our old Norse ancestors of the great Allfather of men. But with this august being was associated a progeny of lesser gods, impersonations of the powers of nature. The stern and savage scenery of the Scandinavian mountains and meres, desolate fiords, sombre forests, and swirling maelstroms, gave to the northern superstitions a peculiarly weird and awful character. The gods were incarnations of savage force and waged incessant war with the *Jotuns* or giants—Frost, Fire, and Tempest. Yet Balder, the beautiful, the Sun-god, who quickens with his smile the dead world to life from the icy rigours of winter, is a nobler conception than the far-darting Phœbus Apollo, and the stern virtues of Odin and Thor shame the vices of Jupiter and Mars.

The religion of the North seems to us to have been instinct with a nobler ethical spirit and a purer morality than the sensuous worship of beauty of the soft and sunny isles of Greece. Hence, in the providence of God, the vigorous Gothic races were chosen to supplant the effete civilization of the South, and to become the fathers of modern Europe. The noble Anglo-Saxon and Teutonic civilization of the world to-day, the foster parent of social order, stable government, and religious liberty, is the result of the religion of the Bible grafted upon the sturdy stock of that old Norse ancestry whose honest blood flows in all our veins. Many elements of our character and history, of our popular belief and folk-lore have their roots far back in that ancient past. In the very names of the days of the week, the memories of Thor and Woden, of Friga and Tuesco, are perpetuated. It is especially befitting that the sons of "that true North" of which the English laureate has sung should become familiar with the traditions which tell how the worship of the "White Christ" took the place of the superstitions of the dark Odin.

A monkish legend records that as the Emperor Charlemagne was once banqueting at Narbonne, some strange swift barks were seen gliding into the harbour. None knew whence they came, but the company surmised that the crew were either Jewish, African, or British traders. The keen eye of the great Emperor soon perceived that this was no friendly visit. From the window he gazed long upon the hostile barks, and the bystanders, continues the legend, observed tears in his eyes. At length, breaking the silence, he remarked, "It is not with merchandise that yonder vessels are laden. They bear most terrible enemies. It is not for myself that I am weeping, but to think that even while I am yet alive they have dared to approach these shores. What will they not do when I am dead?"

The fears of the far-seeing Emperor were only too well founded. Under the degenerate kings of the Carlovingian line,—Charles the Bald, Charles the Fat, Charles the Simple, and the other unworthy successors of Charles the Great—the piratical fleets of the Norseman ravaged the coasts, sailed up the rivers, sacked the towns and laid waste the fair fields of France.

"Take a map," writes Sir Francis Palgrave,* " and colour with vermilion the provinces, districts, and shores which the Northmen visited, as the record of each invasion. The colouring will have to be repeated more than ninety times successively before you arrive at the conclusion of the Carlovingian dynasty. Furthermore, mark by the usual symbol of war, two crossed swords, the localities where battles were fought by or against the pirates; where they were defeated or triumphant, or where they pillaged, burned, destroyed; and the valleys and banks of the Elbe, Rhine, and Moselle, Scheldt, Meuse, Somme, and Seine, Loire, Garonne, and Adour, the inland Allier and all the coasts and coastlands between estuary and estuary, and the countries between the riverstreams will appear bristling as with *chevaux-de-*

* History of Normandy and England, vol. i. p. 419.

frise. The strongly-fenced Roman cities, the venerated abbeys, and their dependent *bourgades*, often more flourishing and extensive than the ancient seats of government, the opulent seaports and trading towns, were all equally exposed to the Danish attacks, stunned by the Northmen's approach, subjugated by their fury."

Similar has been the history of Britain; and forms of speech, local names, seafaring instincts and many other characteristics give evidence of the frequent invasions and permanent influence of the stern sea-kings and their stormy followers. It is the strain of wild viking blood in the veins of her sailor sons that gives to Britain the empire of the waves, and flaunts her flag in every zone.

While these rude Northmen were thus extending their conquests from Iceland to Sicily, and even menacing Byzantium and Rome, there were men of the South who achieved over their victors more glorious victories than those of any sea-king of them all. Serge-clad missionary monks, with no weapons but their cross and missal, braved the wrath of the heathen to bring them to Christ. One of the most notable of these was Anskar, the Apostle of Denmark. He was born near Amiens in the first year of the ninth century, and even in childhood manifested an intense religious enthusiasm. While Anskar was still in his early youth, the Emperor **Charlemagne** died, and the story of his strange entombment profoundly affected the mind of the lad then an acolyte in the Abbey of Corbey. Deep were his searchings of heart as the monks whispered with bated breath in the cloisters of the Abbey, how the dead monarch was ensepulchred "sitting in his curule chair, clad in his silken robes, ponderous with broidery, pearls, and orfray, the imperial diadem on his head, his closed eyelids covered, his face swathed in the death-clothes, girt with his baldric, the ivory horn slung in his scarf, his good sword 'Joyeuse' by his side, the Gospel-book open on his lap, musk and amber and sweet spices all around."* The youthful acolyte vividly realized the power of the great Conqueror who knocks alike at the palace of kings and the cottage of the peasant† and the solemn question was forced upon his thought, "What shall it profit a man if he shall gain the whole world and lose his own soul?" He devoted himself with a new and intenser consecration to a religious life, and a few years later he embraced with joy the opportunity of proceeding as a missionary to the country of the yet pagan **Jutes** and **Danes**.

* PALGRAVE.—History of Normandy and England, vol. i. p. 518.

† Pallida **Mors** æquo pulsat pede pauperum tabernas Regumque turres.—HOR. *Ad. L. Sextium.*

After successful labours in Schleswig, he with a companion in labour pressed on with impassioned zeal to preach the Gospel amid the fiords and valleys of Sweden. But fierce Norse pirates captured the vessel, plundered the missionaries, and barely allowed them to escape with their lives. Undeterred by disaster, they reached the neighbourhood of Stockholm and won converts to the cross even in this stronghold of heathenism. Anskar, now a bishop, made Hamburg the centre of his diocese and redeemed from slavery many Christian youths, captured by the pirates. A heathen invasion, however, ravaged his diocese, pillaged and burned his church and monastery, and drove the missionaries as homeless fugitives amid the meres and marshes of the wild Baltic strand. "The Lord gave, and the Lord hath taken away, and blessed be the name of the Lord," exclaimed the exiled bishop as he took his last look at the ruins of his devastated church. He strengthened his heart with the prophetic thought, "Whatso we have striven to accomplish for the glory of Christ shall yet, by God's grace, bring forth fruit; until the name of the Lord is made known to the uttermost ends of the earth."*

And Anskar lived to see abundant fruit of his labours. Through the influence of such faith and

* Vita S. Anskarii cap. xxiv.

zeal even the rude pirates of the North were led to repentance for sin and obedience to Christ. To the Saint they even ascribed miraculous powers. But these he himself disclaimed. "One miracle," he said, "I would, if worthy, ask the Lord to grant me; that is that by His grace He would make me a good man."

Only one source of disquietude, writes his biographer, troubled his last hours—that he had not been counted worthy to die as a martyr for his Lord. But his forty years of missionary toil and peril and suffering had been a living martyrdom that claims, across the centuries, our loving reverence and admiration.

It was not, however, till the following century that Christianity was established in Norway. Several previous attempts at its introduction were made, which were frustrated by the bitterness of the pagan persecution. One of these sprang from our own Anglo-Saxon Church. Hacon, the son of Harold the Fair-haired, King of Norway, was brought up at the court of our English Athelstan. He was there baptized and nurtured in the Christian faith. Succeeding to the throne of Norway, he sought to establish the Christian religion; and is remembered in history as Hacon the Good. At the Frostething, or assembly of jarls and chieftains, he proposed that all should "be baptized, believe in one God, and Christ the son of Mary, abstain from heathen sacrifices, and keep the Christian feasts." The pirates and the heathen faction strenuously opposed this apostacy from the old gods, and Hacon died without accomplishing much more than grafting some Christian superstitions upon the pagan Yule-tide feasts, traces of which still remain in the festivities of Christmas.

The Constantine of the North who made Christianity the religion of Norway, was King Olaf. This conversion he effected in true viking fashion by sturdy blows and battles, rather than by the more potent influence of reason and conviction. Hence that conversion exerted relatively little restraint over the warlike instincts of the nation, and it long continued by piracy and invasion to be the terror and the scourge of Europe.

Olaf was, for those days, a great traveller. He had visited the stormy Hebrides, England, Germany, Russia, and even far-off Greece and Byzantium. In Germany he met a stalwart priest, Thangbrand by name, who subsequently became his fellow-labourer in the conversion of Norway. The martial ecclesiastic won the heart of the viking by the strange gift of a shield on which was embossed in gold the figure of our Saviour on the Cross. In one of his many voyages Olaf touched at the Scilly Islands, where he was taught by a venerable hermit the mysteries of the Christian faith and was baptized with all his pirate crew. Repairing to Ireland, he married, in Dublin, the sister of the Danish king of that country, who had previously embraced Christianity. Full of zeal for the conversion of his native country, he sailed with his warrior crew for Norway. The story of his labours and success is chronicled in runic rhymes in the "Heimskringla" of Snorri Sturlason, the Icelandic poet. The stirring tale has been repeated by Longfellow in a poem full of martial fire and vigour, "The Saga of King Olaf." From this, in illustration of our subject, we shall quote freely.

As the brave sea-king approached the rugged coast of Norway, he heard, or thought he heard, above the grinding of the glaciers and the rending of the ice floes, the stern challenge of Thor:

'I am the God Thor,
I am the War God,
I am the Thunderer!
Here in my Northland,
My fastness and fortress,
Reign I forever!

" Force rules the world still,
Has ruled it, shall rule it;
Meekness is weakness,
Strength is triumphant,
Over the whole earth
Still it is Thor's-day!

"Thou art a God, too,
  O Galilean!
And thus single-handed
Unto the combat,
Gauntlet or Gospel,
Here I defy thee!"

Over the sea-swell came the stern defiance and fell upon ears that gave it eager welcome—so the ancient Skald represents under outward form the subjective phenomena of mind:

And King Olaf heard the cry,
Saw the red light in the sky,
  Laid his hand upon his sword,
As he leaned upon the railing,
And his ships went sailing, sailing
  Northward into Drontheim fiord.

There he stood as one who dreamed;
And the red light glanced and gleamed
  On the armour that he wore;
And he shouted, as the rifted
Streamers o'er him shook and sifted,
  "I accept thy challenge, Thor!"

Thus came Olaf to his own,
When upon the night wind blown
  Passed that cry along the shore;
And he answered, while the rifted
Streamers o'er him shook and drifted,
  "I accept thy challenge, Thor!"

So Olaf set to work in stern warrior fashion to extirpate idolatry by the strong arm and sharp sword. "I command," he declared, at a stormy

Husting of the jarls and thanes, "that all Norway become Christian or die." As the Saga records it:

> King Olaf answered: "I command
> This land to be a Christian land;
> Here is my Bishop who the folk baptizes!"
>
> There in the temple, carved in wood,
> The image of great Odin stood,
> And other gods, with Thor supreme among them.
>
> King Olaf smote them with the blade
> Of his huge war-axe, gold-inlaid,
> And downward shattered to the pavement flung them.
>
> King Olaf from the doorway spoke:
> "Choose ye between two things, my folk,
> To be baptized or given up to slaughter!"
>
> And seeing their leader stark and dead,
> The people with a murmur said,
> "O King, baptize us with thy holy water!"
>
> So all the Drontheim land became
> A Christian land in name and fame,
> In the old gods no more believing and trusting.

In carrying out this short and easy method with pagans, Olaf had a worthy ally in the priest Thangbrand, a notable specimen of the Church *militant* of the period. He is thus described in the Saga:

> All the prayers he knew by rote,
>   He could preach like Chrysostome
> From the Fathers he could quote,
>   He had even been at Rome.
>   A learned clerk,
>   A man of mark,
> Was this Thangbrand, Olaf's priest.

Olaf at length declared that he had everywhere made an end of the old idolatry and subdued his kingdom to the religion of the Cross.

> "All the old gods are dead,
> All the wild warlocks fled ;
> But the White Christ lives and reigns,
> And throughout my wide domains
> His Gospel shall be spread !"
>   On the Evangelists,
>   Thus swore King Olaf.
>
> And Sigurd the Bishop said,
> " The old gods are not dead,
> For the great Thor still reigns,
> And among the jarls and thanes
> The old witchcraft still is spread."
>   Thus to King Olaf
>   Said Sigurd the Bishop.

Whereupon Olaf swore a mighty oath that he would conquer all the pagan vikings " or be brought back in his shroud." One of these especially, Raud the Strong, was not only a confirmed idolater but a great warlock and skilled in wizardry as well. "But," the bishop piously remarked, " the Lord is not affrighted at the witchcraft of His foes." Raud lived at Salten Fiord, where so dangerous was the swirling tideway that it was more dreaded than even the terrible maelstrom itself. A violent tempest, raised, Olaf believed, by the evil art of Raud, prevented his landing. But the bishop offered prayers and the choristers chanted psalms and swung their censers.

> On the bow stood Bishop Sigurd,
> In his robes like one transfigured,
> And the crucifix he planted
>   High amidst the rain and mist;
>
> Then with holy water sprinkled
> All the ship; the mass-bells-tinkled;
> Loud the monks around him chanted,
>   Loud he read the Evangelist.
>
> As into the Fiord they darted,
> On each side the water parted;
> Down a path like silver molten
>   Steadily rowed King Olaf's ships.
>
> Steadily burned all night the tapers,
> And the White Christ through the vapours
> Gleamed across the Fiord of Salten,
>   As though John's Apocalypse.
>
> Then King Olaf said; "O Sea-king!
> Little time have we for speaking;
> Choose between the good and evil;
>   Be baptized, or thou shalt die!"
>
> But in scorn the heathen scoffer
> Answered: "I disdain thy offer;
> Neither fear I God nor Devil;
>   Thee and thy Gospel I defy!"

Dire was the conflict that followed, but it ended in the total discomfiture of the heathen and the enforced conversion, nominal at least, of the whole surrounding country.

> Then baptized they all that region,
> Swarthy Lap and fair Norwegian,
> Far as swims the salmon, leaping
> > Up the streams of Saltenfiord.
>
> In their temples Thor and Odin
> Lay in dust and ashes trodden,
> As King Olaf, onward sweeping,
> > Preached the Gospel with his sword.

At the Yule-tide feast King Olaf sat with his berserks strong, drinking the nut-brown ale. It was a half-pagan assembly and the song of the Skald and shouts of the berserks were more in praise of Odin than of Christ. The choleric king was prompt to vindicate the honour of his Lord.

> Then King Olaf raised the hilt
> Of his sword, cross-shaped and gilt,
> > And said, "Do not refuse;
> Count well the gain and loss,
> Thor's hammer or Christ's cross:
> > Choose!"
>
> And Halfred the Skald said, "This,
> In the name of the Lord, I kiss,
> > Who on it was crucified!"
> And a shout went round the board,
> "In the name of Christ the Lord,
> > Who died!"

But not by such methods as these was the conversion of Norway to be effected. By the word of the Gospel not by the sword of the warrior were the souls of men to be brought into subjection to the obedience of Christ Jesus. We would not, of course, expect in the wild viking the toleration of the philosopher, the wisdom of the sage, nor the meekness of the saint. But it was not for this man of blood to build the house of the Lord. Nevertheless, he might, like David, prepare the way for that sublime result. The wise Master-Builder often uses strange means, and "God fulfils Himself in many ways."

The end of this stormy life was in keeping with its wild career. "Worsted in a tremendous engagement with the united forces of Denmark and Sweden, rather than yield to his enemies, he flung himself into the sea, and sank beneath the waves." This was about the year 1000. His was the true viking soul. His life-wish was fulfilled. He died, as he had lived, on the sea.

> And the young grew old and gray,
> And never more, by night nor day,
> In his kingdom of Norroway
>   Was King Olaf seen again.

Far away in the convent of Drontheim—so runs the Saga—the Abbess Astrid knelt in prayer upon the floor of stone. And above the tempest, amid the darkness she heard a voice as of one who answered; and in solemn cadence it chanted this response to the challenge of Thor:

"It is accepted,
The angry defiance,
The challenge of battle!
It is accepted,
But not with the weapons
Of war that thou wieldest.

"Cross against corslet,
Love against hatred,
Peace-cry for war-cry!
Patience is powerful;
He that o'ercometh
Hath power o'er the nations!

"Stronger than steel,
Is the sword of the Spirit;
Swifter than arrows
The life of the truth is;
Greater than anger
Is love and subdueth!

"The dawn is not distant,
Nor is the night starless;
Love is eternal!
God is still God, and
His faith shall not fail us;
Christ is eternal."

Another Olaf, remembered in history as Olaf the Saint,* succeeded the wild viking. He invited Christian clergy to the country, and endeavoured to banish paganism from his realm.

* The Church of St. Olaves in London, as well as others in Ireland and even in distant Constantinople, commemorated his name.

But it still lingered in secluded valley and lonely forest, and the heathen faction stirred up perpetual revolt. The King testified his sincerity by permitting none to fight under his standard save those who would receive baptism and wear upon their shield the sign of the cross. In his last battle against the heathen he gave the war-cry "Forward, Christ's-men!" but he was himself defeated and slain.

When Canute the Dane seated himself upon the throne of England and wedded an English spouse, he sent Christian missionaries to evangelize his Scandinavian possessions. Schools and monasteries arose, learning and civilization were diffused, and the worship of Thor and Odin gradually faded away, as the shades of midnight before the dawn of day.

The Scandinavian peninsula early embraced the Reformed Faith and in the Great Gustavus presented a bulwark of Protestantism against the aggressions of Rome. Under the domination of a State Church, nearly devoid of spiritual life, Evangelical religion almost died out in the land. But English and American Methodism have successful missions in that country, and with the establishment of Sunday-schools and the increased circulation of the Scriptures are bringing rich and spiritual blessings to that old historic land.

The conversion of Eastern Europe was the result of the missionary effort of the Byzantine Church. In the ninth century the Bulgarians occupied the whole of that territory, which having been long usurped by the Turks, has been at length restored to them by the recent conquests of Russia. During a war with the Byzantine Empire in the ninth century a Bulgarian princess was captured. While a hostage at Constantinople she adopted the Christian faith. On her ransom and return home, she induced her brother, the reigning prince, to become also a Christian. Methodius, a Byzantine monk, at his request, adorned the walls of his palace with a painting of the Last Judgment. So vivid was the representation of the fate of the heathen, that many of the Bulgarians put away their idols and received Christian baptism.

THE CONVERSION
OF
RUSSIA AND PRUSSIA.

THE CONVERSION OF RUSSIA AND PRUSSIA.

THE conversion of Eastern Europe was the missionary trophy of the Byzantine Church. During a war with the Byzantine Empire in the ninth century, a Bulgarian princess was captured. While a hostage at Constantinople she adopted the Christian faith. On her ransom and return home, she induced her brother, the reigning prince, to become also a Christian. Methodius, a Byzantine monk, at his request, adorned the walls of his palace with a painting of the Last Judgment. So vivid was the representation of the fate of the heathen, that many of the Bulgarians put away their idols and received Christian baptism.

In the vast Scythian wilds and steppes of the Don and Volga, the Russian kingdom was now being established. In the year 955 the princess Olga made a visit to the city of Constantine, and was so impressed by what she saw and heard that she embraced the Christian religion. On her return she endeavoured to induce her son, the reigning monarch, to become partaker of the like precious faith. He was a stern warrior and refused to bow his neck to the Christian yoke. His son, Vladimir, however, was made of more penetrable stuff. A picture of the Last Judgment shown him by a Greek missionary profoundly affected his imagination. "Happy are those who are on the right," he exclaimed; but, with a sigh, he continued, " woe to the sinners who are on the left." " If thou wishest," said the missionary, " to enter with the just who are on the right, you must believe and be baptized." " I will wait awhile," said this Russian Agrippa, but, unlike Agrippa, he diligently studied the Christian religion, and sent ambassadors to the great city of Constantinople to learn its rites and doctrines. " Let them see," said the Emperor Basil Porphyrogenitus, "the glory of our God," and they witnessed the grand festival of St. John Chrysostom, in the great church of St. Sophia.

Even now, its glorious frescoes and mosaics covered and defaced by Moslem iconoclasm and perverted to the superstitions of a Turkish mosque, this vast structure is the sublimest, as it is the oldest temple of Christian origin on the face of the earth. Soon may its swelling dome again re-echo the hallowed accents of Christian worship instead of the vain repetitions of the mufti! The Russian ambassadors were awe-stricken and profoundly impressed. The multitude of lights, the chanting of the hymns, the gorgeous procession of deacons, sub-deacons, and acolytes, and then the prostration of the congregation with the cry "Kyrie

Eleison! Christe Eleison!—Lord have mercy upon us! Christ have mercy upon us!" filled their souls with sacred emotion.

"We know not," said the envoys on their return, "whether we were not in heaven; in truth it would be impossible on earth to find such riches and magnificence. There, in very truth, God has His dwelling with men. No one who has tasted sweets will afterwards take that which is bitter, nor can we any longer abide in heathenism."

Soon Prince Vladimir embraced the Christian faith, and with it the hand of the Princess Anne, sister of the Byzantine emperor, as his royal consort. The huge idol, Peroun, was ignominiously dragged from its temple at a horse's tail and thrown into the Dnieper. "The people," writes the Russian historian, "at first followed their idol down the stream, but very soon gave over when they found that it had no power to help itself."

Vladimir, after the manner of his age, commanded the immediate baptism of his people. "Whoever, on the morrow," ran the proclamation, "shall not repair to the river, whether rich or poor, I shall hold him for my enemy." The whole population therefore, with facile obedience, transferred their allegiance from the gods of their fathers to the God of their king. They flocked in crowds to the Dnieper, and there, says the historian, "some stood in the water up to their necks, others up to their breasts, holding their young children in their arms, while the priests read the prayers from the shores, naming at once whole companies by the same name." It was a strange sight and exhibited little of the intellectual conviction and moral change and Scriptural faith which we justly deem the very essence of conversion. Nevertheless, the lowest form of Christianity is infinitely better than the highest form of paganism, and there may have been the germs of true faith in the hearts of these rude people. The king himself seems to have correctly apprehended the only source of all spiritual help. "O great God," he exclaimed, "who hast made heaven and earth, look down upon thy new people; grant unto them, O Lord, to know thee the true God, as thou hast been made known to Christian lands, and confirm in them a true and unfailing faith; and assist me, O Lord, against my enemy that opposes me, that, trusting in thee and in thy power, I may overcome all his wiles."

In that old city of Kieff, on the site of the temple of the idol-god, was erected the stately Church of St. Basil, "which became henceforward," says Stanley, "the Canterbury of the Russian Empire."[*]

During the mediæval centuries the Sclavonic races occupied the whole of Eastern Europe from

---

[*] "Eastern Churches," p. 409.

the Caspian and the Black Sea to the Baltic. On the banks of the Elbe, Oder, and Saale, dwelt a Sclavic tribe of a fierce and turbulent disposition known as the Wends. The planting of Christianity among this pagan people was accompanied by an illustrious martyrdom, that of John bishop of Mecklenburg. He was one of those zealous and intrepid Irish missionaries who crusaded through Europe in a holy war to conquer the kingdoms for Christ, not with the sword of steel but with the sword of the Spirit, which is the Word of God. His labours among the wild Wends were unusually successful, and thereby provoked the hostility of the pagan priests. He was beaten cruelly with clubs, and when he refused to deny his faith, his inhuman persecutors cut off his hands, his feet and his head. His body was cast into the street for every trampling foot to spurn. His head was impaled upon a pole and borne in triumph to the temple of the pagan deity.

But not thus is the religion of the cross destroyed. Like the sweet rosemary and thyme that, bruised beneath trampling feet, give out their richer fragrance and are more deeply rooted in the earth, so the doctrines of Jesus can never be crushed. A spiritual essence, an immortal life is theirs. The blood of the martyrs is evermore the seed of the Church. Worthy successors burned to emulate the zeal and toil and sufferings of the martyr-missionary. St. Vicelin, Bishop of Oldenburg, with a band of earnest laymen and ecclesiastics, " formed themselves into a fraternity," writes the historian of the mission, " who vowed to devote their lives to prayer and charity, to visit the sick, relieve the poor, and especially labour for the conversion of the Wends." For nine years this pious band toiled on amid obstacles of every kind. But they were at length able to record souls rescued from pagan darkness, and brought to the light of the Gospel. By such pious toil was the torch of truth kept burning brightly and passed on from hand to hand amid the gathering gloom of the long dark ages of Europe, and thus was the wild Wendish land conquered for Christ.

The character of the Prussians from very early times has been one of indomitable energy and relentless persistence. The great Frederick snatching victory after victory from an alliance of nations leagued against him, and the stern Chancellor Bismarck welding by his Titanic energy the Teutonic kingdoms into a United Germany, and conquering the enemies of his country by the lavish expenditure of " blood and iron," are but characteristic types of the Prussian race at the dawn of missionary endeavour. Dark and stern superstitions, and bloody and cruel rites, including even human sacrifice, intensified their innate ferocity and their rough heathen manners. Yet in this unpromising field—on this stony ground—there were not wanting Christian missionaries to sow the good seed of the kingdom and to water it with their blood. One of the earliest and most notable of these was Adalbert, bishop of Prague. He lived in the closing years of the first millennium of the Christian era, when the general expectation of Europe was looking for the end of the world, the destruction of the wicked, and the glorious establishment of the kingdom of Christ.

This feeling found expression in that grand old hymn which has passed down to us through the ages:

> The world is very evil,
>   The times are waxing late,
> Be sober and keep vigil,
>   The Judge is at the gate:
> The Judge who comes in mercy,
>   The Judge who comes with might,
> Who comes to end the evil,
>   Who comes to crown the right.

Impelled by true missionary zeal Adalbert sought to win to the Gospel, before the awful and impending day of doom, the wild pagan tribes of Bohemia, Hungary, and Poland. As the time of the world's probation, as he deemed, grew shorter and shorter, his zeal redoubled, and he resolved to penetrate the hitherto unexplored heathenesse of Prussia. In the year 997 he reached the town of Dantzig, on the marches of Poland. Here his labours were attended with much success, and he pressed on with two companions in a small boat to the still wilder region in the neighbourhood of Konigsberg. Their landing was opposed by the natives, who fell upon them with clubs, and Adalbert, while chanting the Psalter, fell stunned to the bottom of the boat. They managed, however, to escape. But no thought of turning back seems to have entered their minds. They still proceeded on their journey and soon came to one of the native villages. The chief of the tribe received them into his house and summoned his tribesmen to hear the message of the strangers.

"I am come to seek your salvation," said the missionary to the assembled multitude. "The gods whom ye worship are deaf and dumb, and blind. I come to bid you turn from these false idols to the worship of the one true God, Maker of heaven and earth and of all that are therein, besides whom there is no other God. If ye will believe in Him and be baptized in His name, ye shall receive hereafter eternal life and partake, in the mansions He has prepared for them that love and fear Him, of everlasting joy." But this blessed evangel aroused only their wrath and rage. Like the murderers of the proto-martyr, they were cut to the heart and gnashed on them with their teeth. "Away with such fellows from our land," they exclaimed, "These are they who cause our crops to fail, our trees to wither, our flocks and herds to sicken and die. Let them fly at once, or death shall be their doom."

Seeking those who would heed their message, Adalbert and his companions made their way along the bleak and barren Baltic strand. If they suffered their hair to grow after the manner of the country, and laid aside their ecclesiastical garb, and took to working with their hands, the missionaries thought that they might overcome the prejudices of the people and in time win a way to their hearts and bring them to the truth But God willed it otherwise. As they slept in the forest, Adalbert received in a dream what he considered a premonition of his martyrdom. He hailed it with joy and proceeded on his journey with psalms and prayers and praises to God. When weary with the way, he lay down to sleep upon the ground as calmly as a child on his mother's knee. Soon they were aroused by the fierce onset of a crowd of the savage inhabitants of the district, who instantly made them prisoners and clamoured for their blood.

"Be not troubled," said Adalbert to his companions in tribulation. "We know for whom we are thus called to suffer, even for our Lord. His might surpasses all might, His beauty exceeds all beauty, His grace transcends all expression. What can be a nobler death than to die for Him?" Scarcely had he spoken when a pagan priest advanced from the infuriate mob and transpierced him with a lance. Others of the pagans rushed forward and buried their spears in his bosom. "Thus," adds the chronicler, "raising his eyes to heaven, and offering up prayers for his murderers, Adalbert perished on the 23rd of April, A.D. 997."

That brave death on the shores of the Baltic Sea, eight hundred and eighty years ago, still thrills our hearts across the centuries. Smitten by the accolade of martyrdom the heroic missionary has been exalted to the loftiest peerage of the skies. He has joined that great company of glorious confessors before the throne, who wave their palm of victory and wear for evermore, not earth's wreath of laurel nor its crown of gold, but the crown of life, starry and unwithering, that shall never pass away.

> There is a record traced on high,
> That shall endure eternally;
> The angel standing by God's throne
> Treasures there each word and groan;
> And not the martyr's speech alone,

> But every wound is there depicted,
> With every circumstance of pain—
> The crimson stream, the gash inflicted—
> And not a drop is shed in vain.*

So sang the Christian poet Prudentius in the fourth century, and still is the glorious promise true: "The Lord knoweth them that are His." The names of the "great army of martyrs," though forgotten by men are remembered by God; though unrecorded on earth's scroll of fame, they are written in the Lamb's Book of Life.

Inspired by the heroic example of Adalbert and burning to emulate his zeal, his sufferings, and if need be his death, Bruno, the Court chaplain of the Emperor Otho III., left the pomp and splendour of the palace for the perils of the Prussian wilderness. Within twelve months he and his eighteen companions had all followed the brave bishop to the skies by the same glorious but bloodstained path of martyrdom. They made more conquests by their deaths than by their lives. In them was

---

* Inscripta Christo pagina immortalis est,
Excepit adstans angelus coram Deo.
Et quæ locutus martyr, et quæ pertulit :
Nec verbum solum disserentis condidit,
Omnis notata est sanguinis dimensio,
Quæ vis doloris, quive segmenti modus :
Guttam cruoris ille nullam perdidit.
     —Prudentius—*Peristephanon.*

again fulfilled the experience of the early Christians described by Tertullian: "Kill us, rack us, condemn us, grind us to powder; our numbers increase in proportion as you mow us down."* Again and again the forlorn hope of the army of Christendom rushed upon the threatened deaths of pagan persecution till the strongholds of heathenism were forced, the idols utterly destroyed, their worship abolished, and the praises of the true God banished the service of those gods that be no gods.

Yet paganism died hard. There were from time to time uprisings of the heathen party and reactions toward the worship of their ancestors. In one of these, as late as the thirteenth century, three hundred churches and chapels in Prussia were destroyed, and many Christians were put to death.

A military order, the "Brethren of the Sword," with which was merged the "Tuetonic Knights," was enrolled for the purpose of extirpating heathenism from its last strong holds in Europe. For forty years—A.D. 1240 to A.D. 1290—an armed crusade was waged against the lawless ritters who united paganism and plundering to the sore disquietude of the Christian populations. Churches and abbeys, monasteries and schools, were multiplied, and the Christian religion at length universally prevailed.

* Tertullian, *Apology*, cap. 50.

Then came the glorious Lutheran Reformation, emancipating the souls of men from the errors and thraldom of Rome. All Prussia became Protestant, and a bulwark of Protestantism in the stormy conflicts that accompanied this great political as well as religious re-organization of Europe. To day it is the most stubborn barrier, and in the person of Bismarck presents the most relentless opponent to that aggressive Ultramontanism that would, if it could, again bring all kings and peoples under the civil as well as religious denomination of the Pope of Rome.

RAYMOND LULLI
THE MARTYR OF TUNIS.

RAYMOND LULLI THE MARTYR OF TUNIS.

> "Like as the armèd knyghte,
>   Appointed to the fielde,
> With this world will I fighte,
>   And fayth shal be my shylde.
>
> 'Fayth is that weapon stronge,
>   Which will not fayle at nede
> My foes therefore among,
>   Therewith wyl I procede."—*Anne Askewe.*

ONE of the strangest phenomena in history is the rapid spread of Mahometanism in the seventh and eighth centuries. Within a hundred years from the hegira of the False Prophet, the dark and gloomy fanaticism of which he was the founder had extended its baleful shadow from Bokhara to Cordova, from the Indus to the Loire. Its fierce and fiery energy swept away the corrupt Christianity of the East, save some lingering remnants in the secluded Nestorian valleys, in the Armenian monasteries and among the mountains of Abyssinia.

But the rapid expansion of the caliphate exhausted the native population and led to political divisions. Hence its glory was but transient. It contained the germs of its own dissolution, and these soon began to develop. It was like some gorgeous flower, which rapidly expands, soon reaches its full bloom, and then as swiftly fades; or like the fair and fragile maidens of the East who attain a splendid though precocious maturity, but soon become faded and withered.

Sweeping like a tornado over northern Africa on their fiery, desert barbs, the cloud of Mussulman cavalry paused but briefly at the Straits of Gades, and planted the crescent on European soil, there to wage deadly conflict with the cross for eight long centuries. Filling the land like an army of locusts, they found slight barriers in the Pyrenees, but swarmed across their rugged heights, till the fertile plains of France, from the Garonne to the Rhone, became subject to the sway of the Caliphs.

It was an hour of most eminent peril to Europe. Its future destiny was in the balance. It was the crisis of fate for the entire West. Would the conquering tide roll on and overwhelm the nascent nationalities that were everywhere struggling into life, or was the period of its ebb at hand? Should European cities bristle with a grove of minarets or with a forest of spires? Should the superstitions of the mufti and the Saracenic mosque supplant the worship of Christ beneath cathedral dome? Should the son of Abdallah or the Son of Mary receive the homage of the West? · Should we to-day—for the destinies of the New as well as the Old World were involved—be wearing the fez or turban and praying toward Mecca, or be Christian freemen? These were some of the questions depending apparently upon the issues of the hour.

The Moors meanwhile press on. They overspread the plains of Burgundy and Aquitaine, and pitch their tents on the banks of the Loire. They are already half-way from Gibraltar, to the north of Scotland, to the Baltic, and to the confines of Russia. But the fiat had gone forth from the Supreme Arbiter of the destinies of the universe: Hitherto shalt thou come and no further! Then, broken like the waters and scattered like the spray, that wave of invasion recoiled from the shock of the Christian chivalry, and ebbed away forever from the fields of *la belle France*. Europe was safe! Charles Martel and the peers and paladins of France smote the infidels as with a hammer of destruction.

Thus checked in mid-career, and their fiery strength exhausted, the Saracens settled down behind the Pyrenean wall. Here they won laurels far more glorious than those of war. In the cultivation of literature, art, and science they led the van of Western nations. When Arabian civilization was at the zenith of its glory in Spain, the rest of

Europe, except a small area around Rome and Constantinople was in a condition of barbarism. While the Frankish Kings travelled in state in a rude cart drawn by oxen, the Saracen Emirs rode through their fair and flourishing provinces on prancing Andalusian chargers richly caparisoned with housings of Cordova leather, with golden stirrups and jewelled bridle, amid the clash of silver cymbals and flashing scimitars of the famed Toledo steel. While European serf wore hose of straw and jerkins of ill-tanned hide, the Arab peasant was clothed with garments of linen, cotton, or woollen, and the nobles in damask stuffs and silks. London and Paris were mere congeries of wretched wooden structures, penetrated by narrow, crooked, dark and miry lanes, seven hundred years after Cordova and Toledo abounded in well-paved and lighted streets and bazaars, adorned with noble marble edifices, mosques, baths, colleges, and fountains.

Upon the fertile *vegas* of Granada and Cordova waved the yellow corn and flashed the golden orange and citron. There, too, gleamed the snowy bolls of the cotton-plant, and glistened the silky plumage of the sugar-cane. The jasmine bowers and rose gardens of Shiraz seemed transplanted to the fairy courts and colonnad of the Alhambra.

While the strongholds of the European sovereigns were little better than stables—unglazed, bare-walled, and rush-strewn—the lieutenants of the Caliphs held their divans in palaces of oriental magnificence, with mosaic floors and ceilings fretted with gold, with shady alcoves and stately colonnades, where painted glass softened the light, Moorish music lulled the senses, musky odours filled the chambers, and fairy fountains cast up their silver spray; where caleducts in the walls cooled the air, and hypocausts underground warmed the water of the bath. Exquisite arabesques, ivory couches, graceful cabinets of sandal or citron inlaid with mother-of-pearl, softest carpets, richest silks, gold, silver, malachite, porcelain, alabaster, miracles of the loom and needle, filligree, and jewellery, attested the Sybaritic luxury of the inhabitants. Yet the lord of all this splendour confessed to have enjoyed only fourteen happy days in his life!

As one walks, to-day, through the deserted halls of the Alhambra, it appears like a scene of enchantment, and we should scarcely feel surprised were its gorgeous vision to vanish into air. The history of its former occupants seems as unreal as a fairy tale. It is remembered chiefly by that splendid ballad literature that recounts the chivalry and heroism of Ruy Gomez and the Cid Campeador. But it is a tale with a tragic ending, as we feel when we stand in imagination upon the hill from which the unhappy Boabdil took his last lingering look at the halls of his fathers. Of this pathetic scene the memory still lives in the name given by the sun-browned Andalusian peasant to this spot—*El ultimo suspiro del Moro*—" The last sigh of the Moor."

The magnificent empire of the Caliphs has long crumbled into dust. The luxury of the court and the debasing sensualism of the seraglio relaxed the nerves of virtue and of valour. A blight and desolation fill up the scene. The Moorish kingdoms of North Africa have relapsed into barbarism. Their great cities have fallen into ruins. A baleful enchantment, like the spell of a malignant magician, seems to have withered the sinews of their strength, and to have dried up the springs of their prosperity. With all their material splendour, they lacked the great conservative influence of Christianity, and their brilliant career ended in degeneracy and decay.

The might of the Saracens, however, was yet unbroken in the thirteenth century, the time of which we are about to write. They had long held possession of the Balearic islands, as well as of Granada, Sicily, and Southern Italy. They swept up to the very gates of Rome. The *Via Sacra* was trodden by unhallowed feet, and the sword of the infidel threatened the heart of Christendom. In the East, barriers of Europe had been broken, and the city of Constantine, of Chrysostom, of Nazianzen, the last refuge of Greek learning, was destined to become the city of the Sultan, of the seraglio, of the janizary—the haunt of intrigue and cruelty and blood.

At Palma, the capital of Majorca, about the middle of the thirteenth century, was born Raymond Lulli, the subject of this sketch. His parents were of noble rank, and the boy was early introduced to the court of Aragon, where he soon rose to the post of seneschal. With the accomplishments and learning, he acquired also the vices of the court. He became as notorious for profligacy as he was famous for wit and poetic genius. For thirty years, he lived a life of guilty pleasure, when he was arrested by a Divine manifestation, like that which smote a Saul of Tarsus to the ground. He beheld a vision, thrice repeated, of the crucified Redeemer, gazing reproachfully upon him, and heard a call summoning him from sin to holiness. "But how can I, defiled with impurity," he exclaims in deep self-condemnation, "rise and enter on a holier life?" "I see, O Lord," he subsequently wrote, "that trees bring forth every year flowers and fruit, each after their kind. But, sinful that I am, for thirty years, I brought forth no fruit, I but cumbered the ground, injurious to myself and noxious to all around."

Nevertheless, he gathered hope from that comfort of the hopeless, the words of Jesus, "Whosoever cometh unto me I will in no wise cast him out." He resolved to give up everything for Christ, to make his life henceforth a sacrifice to Him. And faithfully he fulfilled his pledge. Soon old things passed away, and all things became new. "The flower at the bottom of the long sunless cavern," writes his biographer, "had caught at last the quickening ray of the Sun of Righteousness, and was beginning to expand and put forth its bloom."

After mature deliberation, Lulli resolved to devote his life to the task of proclaiming the message of the cross to the Saracens, the common enemies of Christendom. It will be remembered that this was the age of the crusades for the rescue from the infidel of

"Those holy fields
Over whose acres walked those blessed feet
Which eighteen hundred years ago were nailed,
For our advantage, on the bitter cross."

The feeling of exasperation against the "foul paynim" was intense. It was, therefore, a very magnanimous resolution of Lulli to seek by moral suasion the conversion of those "miscreant hosts" with whom the only argument hitherto had been with mace and battle-axe. With an apprehension, beyond that of his age, of the true nature of moral conquest, he writes: "It seems to me that the Holy Land can be won in no other way than that whereby thou, O Lord Jesus Christ, and thy holy Apostles won it, even by love, and prayer, and shedding of tears and blood. The Holy Sepulchre and the Holy Land can be won far more effectually by proclaiming the word of truth than by force of arms. Let then spiritual knights go thither; let them be filled with the grace of the Holy Spirit. Let them announce to man the sufferings which their dear Lord underwent, and out of love to Him, shed forth their blood, even as He shed His for them."

Lulli conferred not with flesh and blood as he took upon him this apostolate. He sold all his property, made provision for his wife and children, and, assuming the coarse serge garb of a mendicant, went from church to church seeking grace and spiritual aid in the task he had undertaken. He then secured as teacher a Saracen slave, and spent nine years in the diligent study of the Arabic language. His studies, however, were brought to a tragic close. One day the misbelieving Saracen spoke words of blasphemy against the name of Christ. The warrior blood of his ancestry leaped in his veins, and Lulli smote him in the face. The slave, stung to fury, attempted the life of his master. For this he was cast into prison, and there committed suicide. So disastrously ended Lulli's first personal contact with the race for whose conversion he was devoting his life. The conscience-stricken man repaired to the solitude of a mountain for penitence and prayer. Here he was inspired with the design of composing a demonstration of Christian doctrine of such convincing power that the Moslem muftis would be constrained to embrace the true faith. He diligently wrought at his book, and went to Rome and Paris, seeking to enlist the co-operation of the Pope and of the great university of Christendom. He found, however, political intrigues more in favour in high places than the conversion of the Saracens.

Failing to awaken any sympathy with his project, he resolved single-handed and alone to begin his mission among the fierce and fanatical Moslem of Northern Africa. He accordingly took ship from Genoa for Tunis, and his books, papers, and personal effects were placed on board. But now the high courage which had inspired him during long years in the face of danger failed. The perils of torture, imprisonment—perhaps some dreadful form of death—unnerved his soul. Like Jonah, he shrank from the burden of prophecy which he felt laid upon him. His books were removed from the vessel, which sailed without him. But compunctions of keenest remorse now stung his soul. He got no rest day nor night. He felt himself a traitor to his Master, a fugitive from the work to which God had called him. So intense was his mental anguish that it threw him into a violent fever. Though weak in body, yet once more strong in soul, he demanded to be carried on board another ship about to sail. His friends, although convinced that he could not live, yielded to his demand. His strong will asserted its mastery over his feeble frame. Scarce was he out of sight of land when his fever abated and his bodily strength was restored.

On reaching Tunis, Lulli invited the Moslem doctors to a conference or disputation. They responded promptly to the challenge, and a logical tournament, of great skill and persistency on both sides, ensued. The battle revolved about the doctrines of the Trinity and the Divinity of our Lord, which the Imauns, of course, denied. One result, at least, followed—the active persecution of Lulli and his commitment to prison. If they could not confute his arguments, they could at least prevent their diffusion and silence forever in death the voice of the zealous preacher—the last resort of persecution in every age.

At the intercession of one of the Imauns, who

was struck with the courage of the man, the death penalty was commuted to banishment from the country, with the admonition that if ever found in Tunis again he should pay the forfeit by being stoned to death. "But unwilling," says his biographer, "to relinquish the hopes of a lifetime, he managed to return to Tunis unawares, and for three months concealed himself in the neighbourhood of the harbour." As he found, however, no opportunity of inculcating the doctrines of the Christian faith, he resolved to travel from place to place, teaching and preaching whenever and wherever he could. He spent ten years in Southern Europe, Asia, and Northern Africa, lecturing and expounding philosophy in French or Italian universities, arguing with Jews and Mahometans in Minorca, Majorca, Cyprus, and the Ægean Isles, or seeking to reclaim to orthodoxy the heretical sects among the mountains of Armenia.

At length he is found arguing in Arabic with the Moslem literati in the market-place of Bugia, in North Africa. The fanatical populace clamour for his blood and surround him with imprecations on their lips, murder in their eyes, and hands uplifted to stone him to death. He is rescued for the time and admonished of the madness of exasperating the mob. "Death has no terrors," he replies, "for a servant of Christ who is seeking to bring souls to a knowledge of the truth." He was soon, however, thrown into a dungeon, where he languished for six months, befriended only by some Christian merchants. The Moors meanwhile, eager to gain so illustrious a convert, offered him liberty, wealth, high places, and power if he would but abjure the Christian faith. To all these temptations, this dungeon-captive proudly replied: "And I also promise you wealth and honour and everlasting life, if you will forsake your false creed and believe in the Lord Jesus Christ."

Lulli was soon driven from the country, and in his escape, suffered shipwreck. He was now over seventy years of age, but the ardour that animated his prime still glowed within his breast. The same high aspirations still fired his soul. "Once I was rich," he writes; "once I had a wife and children; once I tasted freely of the pleasures of this life. But all these things I gladly resigned that I might spread abroad a knowledge of the truth. I have been in prisons. I have been scourged. For years I have striven to persuade the princes of Christendom to promote the common good of all men. Now, though old and poor, I do not despair. I am ready, if it be God's will, to persevere even unto death." And thus, like Paul the aged, having fought the fight and kept the faith, and ready to be offered up, he went rejoicing to his doom.

Eager to create a new order of knighthood that should reconquer Palestine for Christ, not by deeds of bloody and brute prowess, but by a spiritual knight-errantry of toil and suffering, he urged, and in part procured, the establishment of missionary colleges in various parts of Europe, and of professorships of oriental languages at Paris, Salamanca, and Oxford, the great seats of learning of Christendom.

Although the worn and weary body might well claim repose, the intrepid spirit would brook no surcease of its toil. "Men are wont to die," he writes, "from old age, from the failure of natural warmth, from excess of cold. But thus, if it be thy will, O Lord, thy servant would not wish to die. He would prefer to expire in the glow of love, even as Thou wast willing to die for him. As the needle turns to the north when it is touched by the magnet, so it is fitting, O Lord, that thy servant should turn to love and praise and serve thee, seeing that out of love to him thou didst endure such grievous pangs and sufferings."

He therefore set out on what he must have felt to be, in all probability, his last missionary journey. He crossed once more to Northern Africa, and for a year continued to labour secretly among those who on his former visits had been induced to listen to his teaching. He never grows weary of expatiating on the love of God, as manifested in the incarnation, life, and death of His Son,—"a love," he says," beyond all other love,"—a love which passeth knowledge. This was the ceaseless theme of his daily converse and of his meditation.

"At length," writes his biographer, "longing for the crown of martyrdom, he came forth from his seclusion, and presenting himself openly to the people, proclaimed that he was the same man they had once expelled from the town, and boldly denounced their errors." Like the murderers of St. Stephen, the fanatical mob " ran upon him with one accord and cast him out of the city and stoned him to death." But like that blessed martyr, he, too, beheld by faith the heaven open and the Son of man standing on the right hand of God. As his eyes filmed with the shadows of death, he was enbraved by that beatific vision, and, above the roar of the mob, fell sweetly on his inner ear the welcome from the toils and persecutions of earth to the everlasting rest and reward of the skies. Like a sick child that falls asleep in tears and pain and wakes beneath his mother's kiss— so his world-weary spirit awoke to eternal life beneath the smile of God.

Thus! oh, not *thus!* no type of earth can image that awaking
Wherein he scarcely heard the chant of seraphs round him
    breaking,
Or felt the new immortal throb of soul from body parted,
But felt those eyes alone, and knew,—*my* Saviour! *not* deserted.

The venerable martyr was in his eightieth year. His tragic death took place on the 30th of June, A.D. 1315. The mangled body was tossed contemptuously without the gates of the town and covered beneath a pile of stones. Some of his countrymen obtained permission to gather his bones and with loving care conveyed them for burial to his native land. His voluminous writings were published in ten volumes at Mentz in 1721-42—ponderous tomes of philosophy, the science of the day, and devout meditations on God. But his noblest monument, and that by which he will be longest remembered and most endeared to the heart of Christendom, is his brave life of missionary toil, and his heroic death beneath the walls of that old Moorish town between the Lybian sands and the Sicilian sea.

THE MARTYRS OF CANADA.

It has been sometimes said that Canada is too young a country to possess those historic memories which give such a spell of fascination to older lands. But young as our country is, it presents examples of as noble heroism as have ever graced the annals of any land beneath the sun. Dulac des Ormeaux and his comrades in battle devoted themselves to the rescue of their country at the pass of Carlton on the Ottawa with a self-sacrifice unsurpassed by that of Leonidas and his three hundred at Thermopylæ, or of Horatius at the Sublician Bridge. And in this Province of Ontario the faith and zeal and steadfastness even unto death of the Martyrs of Canada have never been surpassed in the annals of missionary heroism.

That subtle and sinister system which in the sixteenth and seventeenth centuries belted the world with its missions and won renown and execration in almost every land, gained some of its grandest triumphs and exhibited its most heroic spirit in the wilderness of Canada. The Jesuits had numbered as converts hundreds of thousands of baptized pagans in India and the Moluccas, in China and Japan, in Brazil and Paraguay. They almost entirely controlled the religious education of youth in Europe and kept the consciences of kings, nobles, and great ladies, who sought at their feet spiritual guidance and counsel. They had won well-merited fame for their attainments in ancient learning, for modern science, for pulpit eloquence, and for subtle state craft. Under the disguise of a Brahmin, a manderin, an astrologer, a peasant, a scholar, they had compassed the world to make proselytes to Rome. Deciphering ancient manuscripts or inscriptions, sweeping the heavens with the telescope or digging the earth with a mattock, editing the classics or ancient Fathers, or teaching naked savages the *Ave* or *Credo*, they were alike the obedient and zealous servants of their Order, to whose advancement their whole being was devoted. They were at once among the greatest friends of human learning and the most deadly enemies of civil liberty.

But nowhere did the Jesuit missionaries exhibit grander moral heroism or sublimer self-sacrifice, nowhere did they encounter greater sufferings with more pious fortitude, or meet with a more tragical fate than in the wilderness missions of New France. They were the pioneers of civilization, the path-finders of empire on this continent

With breviary and crucifix, at the command of the Superior of the Order at Quebec, they wandered all over the vast country stretching from the rocky shores of Nova Scotia to the distant prairies of the Far West, from the regions around Hudson's Bay to the mouth of the Mississippi River. Paddling all day in their bark canoes, sleeping at night on the naked rock; toiling over rugged portages or through pathless forests; pinched by hunger; gnawed to the bone by cold; often dependent for subsistence on acorns, the bark of trees, or the bitter moss to which they have given their names;* lodging in Indian wigwams whose acrid smoke blinded their eyes and whose obscene riot was unutterably loathsome to every sense; braving peril and persecution and death itself, they persevered in their path of self-sacrifice, for the glory of God,† the salvation of souls, the advancement of their Order, and the extension of New France. "Not a cape was turned, not a river was entered," writes Bancroft, "but a Jesuit led the way."

As early as 1626, Jean de Brebeuf established a mission among the Hurons on the shores of the

* "Jesuits' moss"—*tripe de roche*—a coarse edible lichen which abounds in northern wastes.

† *Ad majorem gloriam Dei*, is the motto of the Order of Jesus.

Georgian Bay. In 1641, Peres Jogues and Raymbault told the story of the Cross to a wondering assembly of two thousand redmen beside the rushing rapids of the Ste. Marie, at the outlet of Lake Superior, five years before Eliot had preached the gospel to the Indians within gunshot of Boston town.

The story of Jogues' subsequent adventures is one of tragic interest. The following summer (1642), returning from Quebec with supplies for the Huron Mission, his party were suprised by the Iroquois on Lake St. Peter and carried prisoners to the Mohawk towns. Every indignity and torture that the human frame can endure was wreaked upon the wretched priest,—a man of gentle birth, delicate culture, and scholarly training—and upon his companions. With mangled hands and bruised and bleeding body, he was dragged in savage triumph from town to town—the sport of wanton boys and cruel squaws. His companions having been murdered or burned at the stake, Jogues wandered through the wintry woods, carved the cross and the name of Jesus on the trees, and lifted his voice in a litany of sorrow. But his soul was sustained by visions of his Divine Master and by the holy joy of being enabled to baptize by stealth no less than seventy Mohawk children.

and thus, as he fondly believed, to snatch their souls from eternal perdition.

After a series of hair-breadth escapes, he was rescued by the Dutch at Fort Orange and was restored to France. Feted and caressed by the Queen of Louis XIII. and by the ladies of the court, he longed to engage once more in his self-sacrificing missionary toils, and with the early spring, took ship again for Canada. Undaunted by the agonies he had endured, he returned to the scene of his sufferings, to establish among the Mohawks the Mission of the Martyrs, as it was prophetically named. "*Iboet non redibo*—I shall go, but I shall not return," he said, with a just presentiment of his fate, as he parted from his friends. He was soon barbarously murdered, and thus received the martyr's starry and unwithering crown, A.D. 1644.

Similar was the fate of Bressani, an Italian Jesuit. Taken prisoner, like Jogues, while on his way to the Huron Mission; scarred, scourged, beaten, mangled, burned, and tortured with hungry dogs fed off his naked body,—he still continued to live. "I could not have believed," he wrote, "that a man was so hard to kill."

"I do not know," he says in his letter to the General of the Order at Rome, "if your Paternity will recognize the writing of one whom you once knew very well. The letter is soiled and ill-written, because the writer has only one finger of his right hand left entire, and cannot prevent the blood from his wounds, which are still open, from staining the paper. His ink is gunpowder mixed with water, and his table is the ground." He, too, was rescued by the Dutch at Fort Orange, returned to France, but eagerly hastened, as if in love with death, back to the scene of his sufferings and his toils.*

The shores of the Georgian Bay present to the voyager upon its waters a picturesque variety of bold headlands, rocky islands of every size and shape, and quiet inlets bordered by the columned forest or the smiling clearing and thriving town or village. The region between Nottawasaga Bay and Lake Simcoe, which is now a rich agricultural district, was, two centuries and a half ago, the home of the numerous and powerful Huron nation of Indians. Much of this region is still covered with what seems to be a virgin forest, yet the plough and

---

* Of the Jesuit missionaries in Canada, not a few earned the honoured title of martyrs and confessors of the faith. Among these were Pères Daniel, Brébeuf, Lalemant, Garnier, Garreau, Jogues, Buteax and Chabanet; and Goûpil, Brulé and Lalande, lay labourers, who died by violence in the service of the mission. De Noue was frozen to death in the snow, and Bressani, Châtelaine, Chaumonot, Couture, and others, endured tortures far worse than death.

THE ROMANCE OF MISSIONS. 93

the axe of the pioneer often bring to light the relics of a former population concerning whom local tradition is silent, and of whom the lingering red men of the present know nothing. Yet in the pages of history live the records of this lost race, written with a fidelity and vigour that rehabilitate the past and bring us face to face with this extinct nation. The three large volumes of *Relations des Jesuites** contain a minute and graphic account by men of scholastic training, keen insight and cultivated powers of observation, of the daily life, the wars and conflicts, the social, and especially the religious, condition of this strange people. As we read these quaint old pages, we are present at the firesides and the festivals of the Huron nation; we witness their superstitious rites and usages, their war and medicine dances, and their funeral customs; and, at length, as the result of the pious zeal of the Jesuit missionaries, their general adoption of Christianity and their celebration of Christian worship.

In the region between the Georgian Bay, Lake Simcoe, and the River Severn, in the year 1639, were no less than thirty-two Huron villages, and

* For forty years, 1632-1672, these *Relations* were annually sent to the Provincial of the Order at Paris. They were collected and published in three large 8vo. volumes by the Canadian Government in 1858. I have closly followed these *Relations* in the text.

about thirty thousand inhabitants. These villages were not mere squalid collections of wigwams, but consisted of well-built dwellings, about thirty or thirty-five feet high, as many wide, and sometimes thirty and even a hundred yards long. They were generally well fortified by a ditch, rampart, and three or four rows of palisades; and sometimes had flanking bastions which covered the front with a cross-fire. The inhabitants were not mere hunting nomads, but an agricultural people, who laid up ample stores of provisions, chiefly Indian corn, for their maintenance during the winter.

It is not within the scope of this paper to describe the planting of the Huron mission, but rather to depict the closing scenes of the forest tragedy.

As early as 1626, Jean de Brebeuf, the apostle of the Hurons had visited, and for three years remained among, these savage tribes. On Kirk's conquest of Quebec, he was recalled, but in 1634, accompanied by Peres Daniel and Davost, he returned under a savage escort to the temporarily abandoned mission. By a tortuous route of nine hundred miles up the Ottawa, and through Lake Nipissing, French River, and the Georgian Bay, they reached the Bay of Penetanguishene. Over four-and-thirty portages, sometimes several miles long, often steep and rugged, through tangled forests and over sharp rocks that lacerated their naked feet, the missionary pioneers helped to bear their bark canoes and their contents. Fifty times they had to plunge into rapids and, wading or stumbling over boulders in the rocky channel, to drag the laden boats against an arrowy stream. With drenched and tattered garments, with weary and fasting frames, with bruised and mangled feet, stung by mosquitoes and venomous insects, they had to sleep on the damp earth or naked rock. "But amid it all," writes Brebeuf, "my soul enjoyed a sublime contentment, knowing that all I suffered was for God."* Separated from his companions and abandoned by his perfidious escort, Brebeuf offered himself and all his labours to God for the salvation of these poor savages,† and pressed through the woods to the scene of his former toil. He found that Brule, a fellow-countryman, had been cruelly murdered in his absence; and, with prophetic instinct, anticipated the same fate for himself, but desired only that it might be in advancing the glory of God. Davost and Daniel soon after arrived, a mission house and chapel were built, and the latter decorated with a few pictures, images,

* "Mon âme ressentoit de très-grands contentmens, considérant que ie suffrois pour Dieu. Brébeuf, *Relation des Hurons*, 1635, p. 26.

† "M'offris a nostre Seigneur, avec tous nos petits travaux, pour le salut de ces pauvres peuples."—*Ib.* 28.

and sacred vessels, brought with much trouble over the long and difficult route from Quebec. Here the Christian altar was reared, surpliced priests chanted the ancient litanies of the Church, whose unwonted sounds awoke strange echoes in the forest aisles, and savage tribes were besought by the death of Christ and the love of Mary to seek the salvation of the Cross.

But by weary years of hope deferred the missionaries' faith was sorely tried. They toiled and preached and prayed and fasted without any apparent reward of their labour. The ramparts of error seemed impregnable. The hosts of hell seemed leagued again them. The Indian "sorcerers," as the Jesuits called the medicine-men, whom they believed to be the imps of Satan, if not, indeed, his human impersonation, stirred up the passions of their tribe against the mystic medicine-men of the pale-faces. These were the cause, they alleged, of the fearful drought that parched the land, of the dread pestilence that consumed the people; the malign spell of their presence neutralized the skill of the hunter and the valour of the bravest warrior. The chanting of their sacred litanies was mistaken for a magic incantation, and the mysterious ceremonies of the mass for a malignant conjury. The cross was a charm of evil potency, blasting the crops and affrighting the thunder-bird that brought the refreshing rain.

The missionaries walked in the shadow of a perpetual peril. Often the tomahawk gleamed above their heads or a deadly ambush lurked for their lives. But beneath the protection of St. Mary and St. Joseph, as they unfalteringly believed, they walked unhurt. The murderous hand was restrained, the death-winged arrow was turned aside ; undismayed by their danger, undeterred by lowering looks and muttered curse, they calmly went on their message of mercy. In winter storms and summer heat, from plague-smitten town to town, they journeyed through the dreary forest, to administer their homely simples to the victims of the loathsome small-pox, to exhort the dying, to absolve the penitent, and, where possible, to hallow with Christian rites the burial of the dead. The wail of a sick child, faintly heard through the bark walls of an infected cabin, was an irresistible appeal to the missionaries' heart. Heedless of the scowling glance or rude insult, they would enter the dwelling and, by stealth or guile, they would administer the sacred rite which, as they thought, snatched an infant soul from endless perdition,—from the jaws of the "Infernal Wolf."* They shared the privations

---

* "Ce loup infernal." Thus, as they phrased it, the dying infants were changed "from little savages to little

and discomforts of savage life; they endured the torments of filth and vermin; of stifling, acrid smoke parching the throat and inflaming the eyes till the letters of the breviary seemed written in blood. Often they had no privacy for devotion save in the dim crypts of the forest, where, carving a cross upon a tree, they chanted their solemn litanies till, gnawed to the bone by the piercing cold, they returned to the reeking hut and foul orgies of pagan superstition.

Yet the hearts of the missionaries quailed not; they were sustained by a lofty enthusiasm that courted danger as a condition of success. The gentle Lalemant prayed that if the blood of the martyrs were the necessary seed of the Church, its effusion should not be wanting. Nor did the mission lack in time that dread baptism. The pious Fathers believed that powers supernal and infernal fought for them or against them in their assault upon the Kingdom of Satan! On the side of Christ, His Virgin Mother, and the blessed Gospel were legions of angels and the sworded seraphim. Opposed to them were all the powers of darkness, aided by those imps of the pit, the dreaded "sorcerers," whom Satan clothed

angels." Of a thousand baptisms in 1639—all but twenty were baptized in immediate danger of death. Two hundred and **sixty** were infants and many more quite young.

with vicarious skill to baffle the efforts of the missionaries and the prayers of the holy Saints. Foul fiends haunted the air, and their demoniac shrieks or blood-curdling laughter could be heard in the wailing of the night wind, or in the howling of the wolves down the dim forest aisles. More dreadful still, assuming lovely siren forms, they assailed the missionary on the side of his human weakness; but at the holy sign of the cross the baneful spell was broken—the tempting presence melted into air.*

Yet with these intensely realistic conceptions of their ghostly foes, the Jesuits shrank not from the conflict with Hell itself. Emparadised in beatific vision, they beheld the glorious palace of the skies prepared, a heavenly voice assured them, for those who dwelt in savage hovels for the cause of God on earth. Angelic visitants cheered their lonely vigils, and even the Blessed Mother of Christ, surrounded by a choir of holy virgins, by her smile of heavenly approbation enbraved their souls for living martyrdom.† Nor were they

* Ragueneau, *Relation des Hurons*, 1649, 24. One chapter of the *Relations* is headed *Du règne de Satan en ces contrées*, which the simple Fathers designated the very fortress and donjon-keep of demons—une des principales fortresses et comme un donjon des Démons.

† *Relation*, 1649, 24.

without previsions of their future sufferings and of the manner in which they should glorify God.

Many years before his martyrdom, Christ crowned with thorns appeared in a vision to Brebeuf, and revealed to him that he also should tread the thorny way of the holy Cross. Again, the Saviour, with an infinite compassion, folded him in a loving embrace, pardoned all his sins, and, with the assurance that he was a chosen vessel to bear his name unto the Gentiles, showed him how great things he must suffer for His name's sake. In a transport of devotion the willing victim exclaimed—" Naught shall separate me from the love of Christ, nor tribulation, nor nakedness, nor peril, nor the sword."* His ardour for martyrdom rising into a passion, he writes, " I feel myself vehemently impelled to die for Christ." "Yea, Lord," he exclaimed, " though all the torments that captives in these lands can undergo in their cruel sufferings should fall on me alone, I offer, with all my heart, to endure them in my own person."†

Indeed he sought by his rigorous penances to make his life a continuous martyrdom. Beneath

* Ragueneau, *Relation des Hurons*, 1649, 23.

† Ouy, mon Dieu, si tous les tourmens que les captifs peuvent endurer en ces pays, dans la cruauté des supplices, devroient tomber sur moy, ic m'y offre de tout mon cœur, et moy seul ie les souffriray. *Ib.* 23.

his hair-shirt he wore an iron girdle, studded with sharp points. Daily, or more often still, he inflicted upon himself unsparing flagellation. His fasts were frequent and austere, and often, in pious vigils, he wore the night away.

Such enthusiasm as that of these empassioned devotees was not without its unfailing reward Inveterate prejudice was overcome, bitter hostility was changed to tender affection, and the worn and faded close black cassock, the cross and the rosary hanging from the girdle, and the wide-brimmed, looped-up hat of the Jesuit missionary became the objects of kind regard instead of the symbols of a dreaded spiritual power. The Indians abandoned their cruel and cannibal practices. Many of them received Christian baptism. In the rude forest sanctuary was broken to savage neophytes the sacred bread which the crowned monarchs of Europe received from the hands of mitred priests beneath the cathedral dome. As at evening the Angelus sounded,

"The bell from its turret
Sprinkled with holy sounds the air, as a priest with his hyssop
Sprinkles the congregation, and scatters blessings among them."

The little children were taught to repeat the *Ave*, the *Credo*, and the *Pater Noster*. Rude natures were touched to human tenderness and pity by the tender story of a Saviour's love; and lawless passions were restrained by the dread menace of eternal flames. Savage manners and unholy pagan rites gave way to Christian decorum and devotion, and the implacable red men learned to pray for their enemies.

That, in some instances at least, the conversion of the Indians was not a merely nominal one but a radical change of disposition, is evinced by the following prayer of a Huron tribe for their hereditary foes, the cruel Iroquois:—" Pardon, O Lord, those who pursue us with fury, who destroy us with such rage. Open their blind eyes; make them to know Thee and to love Thee, and then, being Thy friends they will also be ours, and we shall together be Thy children."* A more signal triumph of grace over the implacable hate of the Indian nature it is difficult to conceive. " Let us strive," exclaimed another convert, "to make the whole world embrace the faith in Jesus."

The scattered missionaries were reinforced by eager recruits drawn across the sea by an impassioned zeal that knew no abatement even unto

---

* "Seigneur, pardonnez à ceux qui nous poursuivent avec tant de fureur, qui nous font mourir avec tant de rage, ouvrez leurs yeux, ils ne voyent goutte; faites qu'ils vous connoissent et qu'ils vous ayment, et alors estans vos amys ils, seront les nostres, et nous serons tous vos enfans." Vincent, *Relation*, 1645, 16.

death. At almost every Indian town was a mission established and consecrated by some holy name. Thus in the Northern half of what is now the County of Simcoe, were the missions of St. Michel, St. Joseph, St. Jean Baptiste, St. Louis, St. Denys, St. Antoine, St. Charles, St. Ignace,* St. François Xavier, Ste. Marie, Ste. Anne, Ste. Agnes, Ste. Catherine, Ste. Cecile, St. Genevieve, Ste. Madeleine, Ste. Therese, and several others. The most important of these was that of Ste. Marie, established in 1640, on a small stream, now known as the River Wye, which flows into Gloucester Bay, itself an inlet of the Georgian Bay, not far from the present town of Penetanguishene. The outlines of the fortification, for it was both fort and mission, may still be traced amid the forest, which has long since overgrown the spot. A wall of combined masonry and palisades, flanked by bastions at the angles, enclosed a space of some thirty by sixty yards, containing a church, a mission residence, a kitchen, and a refectory. Without the walls were a hut for Indian visitors, a hospital for the sick, and a cemetery for the dead. Sometimes as many as sixty white men were assembled at the mission, among whom were

* The frequency of this designation, throughout the whole of New France, attests the veneration in which the founder of the Society of Jesus was held.

eight or ten soldiers, as many hired labourers, about a score of men serving without pay, and as many priests; most of these, however, were generally engaged in the various out-missions. The demands upon the hospitality of Ste. Marie were very great. During the year 1649 as many as six thousand Christian Indians were lodged and fed. But the Fathers bestowed such care on agriculture, sometimes themselves working with spade and mattock, that in 1648 they had provisions laid up sufficient for three years. They had also a considerable quantity of live stock, including fowls, swine, and even horned cattle, brought with infinite trouble through the wilderness.

But this prosperity was destined to be rudely interrupted and to have a tragic close.

The terrible Iroquois, who dwelt to the south of Lake Ontario, in what is now Central New York, the most warlike and cruel of all the Indian races, the scourge and terror alike of the French and English settlements, waged perpetual war against their hereditary foes, the Hurons. Urged by implacable hate, large war parties would travel on snow-shoes through a pathless forest for hundreds of miles to burn and destroy the Huron villages and indiscriminately massacre their inhabitants, not merely the warriors, but the old men, the women, the little children. No distance was too great, no perils too formidable, if they might only glut their thirst for Huron blood. Even single individuals lurked for weeks near the walls of Quebec or Montreal, for the opportunity to win a Huron scalp. With the persistence of a sleuth hound, a small war party of Iroquois travelled twenty days' journey north of the St. Lawrence in mid-winter to attack a Huron camp, and wantonly butchered its inhabitants. The ubiquitous and blood-thirsty wretches infested the forest; lay in ambush at the portages of the Ottawa and St. Lawrence, and sprang, like a tiger on his prey, on the straggling parties of their foes. Their victims they tortured with demoniac cruelty. They hacked the body with knives and shells, scorched it with burning brands, and after, with fiendish ingenuity, exhausting every mode of suffering, in their unhallowed frenzy they devoured the quivering flesh. "They are not mèn but wolves," said a wretched victim of their rage.

This tempest of heathen rage in 1648 was let loose on the Christian missions. The storm burst on the frontier village of St. Joseph, situated not far from the present town of Barrie, on the morning of July 4. This village had two thousand inhabitants, and was well fortified, but most of the warriors were absent at the hunt or on distant journeys. Pere Daniel, who for fourteen years had here laboured in the wilderness, arrayed in the vestments of his office, had just finished the celebration of the mass in the crowded mission chapel, when the dread war whoop of the Iroquois was heard. The painted savages rushed through the unprotected openings in the palisade, murdering all whom they met. Unable to baptize separately the multitude who, hitherto impenitent, now sought this ordinance, Pere Daniel dipped his handkerchief in water and, shaking it over the terrified crowd, exclaimed "My brethren, to-day we shall be in heaven."* Absolving the dying, and baptizing the penitent, he refused to escape. "Fly, brothers," he cried to his flock. "I will die here. We shall meet again in heaven."† Boldly fronting the foe he received in his bosom a sheaf of arrows, and a ball from a deadly arquebuse. "He fell," says the contemporary chronicler, "murmuring the name of Jesus, and yielding joyously his soul to God; truly a good shepherd, who gave his life for his sheep."‡

* " Mes Frères, nous serons aujourdhuy dans le Ciel."— Ragueneau, *Relation des Hurons*, 1649, 3.

† " Fuyez, mes Frères. Pour moy, ie dois mourir icy; nous nous reverrons dans le ciel." *Ib.* 4.

‡ " Il tomba prononçant le nom de Jésus, en rendant heureusement son âme à Dieu, vrayment un bon Pasteur, qui expose et son âme et sa vie pour le salut de son troupeau." *Ib.* 4.

Seven hundred persons, mostly women or children, were captured or killed. The body of the proto-martyr of the Huron Mission was burned to ashes, but his intrepid spirit, it was believed, appeared again among the living, animating their hearts to endure unto the bitter end; and not for one moment did they quail. "We cannot hope," writes Ragueneau, his companion in toil and tribulation, "but to follow in the burning path which he has trod, but we will gladly suffer for the glory of the Master whom we serve."

The next act of this tragedy opens eight months later, in the early spring of 1649. A thousand Iroquois warriors had, during the winter, made their way from near the Hudson River, round the head of Lake Ontario and across the western peninsula to the Huron country. The object of attack was the village of St. Ignace, situated about ten miles northwest of the present town of Orillia. It was completely surprised in the early dawn of March 16th, and taken almost without a blow.* All the inhabitants were massacred, or reserved for cruelties more terrible than death, save three fugitives, who fled half-naked across the snow to the neighbouring town of St. Louis, about three miles off. Most of the inhabitants of St. Louis

* "Quasi sans coup férir."—Ragueneau, *Relation de Hurons*, 1649, 10.

had time to escape before the attack of the Iroquois, but about eighty Huron warriors made a stand for the defence of their homes. With them remained the two Jesuit missionaries, Jean de Brebeuf and Gabriel Lalemant, who, scorning to fly, chose the point of danger among their flock, standing in the breach, the one baptizing the catechumens, the other absolving the neophytes.* The town was speedily taken and burned. The Jesuits, however, were not immediately killed, "being reserved for a more glorious crown,"† but were, with the other captives, driven before their exulting conquerors back to St. Ignace.

Now began a scene of fiendish torture. The missionaries, stripped naked, were compelled to run the gauntlet through a savage mob, frenzied with cruelty, drunk with blood. They received a perfect storm of blows on every part of the body. "Children," said Brebeuf to his fellow captives, "let us look to God. Let us remember that He is the witness of our sufferings, that He will be our exceeding great reward. I feel for you more than for myself. But endure with courage

---

* "L'un éstoit a la brèche baptisant les catechumènes, l'autre donnant l'absolution aux néophytes."—Ragueneau, *Relations des Hurons*, 1649, 11.

† "Dieu les reseruoit à des couronnes bien plus grandes."—*Ib.*

the little that remains of these torments. They will end with our lives, but the glory that follows will continue forever."

The Iroquois, maddened to fury, tore off the nails of their victims, pierced their hands, lacerated their flesh. Brebeuf, of brawny frame and iron thews, and dauntless bearing—the Ajax of the Huron Mission—was the especial object of their rage. On him they wreaked their most exquisite tortures. They cut off his lips, they seared his throat and bleeding gums, they hung a collar of red-hot hatchets around his neck. "But he stood like a rock, unflinching to the last, without a murmur or a groan, his soul even then reposing on God, an object of amazement even to savage stoicism."* The gentle and delicate Lalemant they envelope in bark saturated with pitch, which they fired, seaming his body with livid scars. As the stifling wreaths of smoke arose, he cried, "We are made a spectacle to the world, to angels and to men." In derision of the rite of baptism, which the missionaries had so often administered to others, their savage tormentors poured boiling water on their heads. "We baptize you," they said, "that you may be

* "Souffroit comme un rocher. Sans pousser aucun cry, estonnoit ses bourreaux mesmes; sans doute que son cœur reposoit alors en son Dieu."— Ragueneau, *Relation des Hurons.* 1649. 14.

happy in heaven; for without a good **baptism no one** can be saved."

The dying **martyrs freely** pardoned their foes, praying **God not to** lay these things to their charge. After nameless tortures the human **hyenas scalped** Brebeuf while yet alive. Lalemant endured his sufferings for seventeen hours, **and** died by **the welcome** stroke of a tomahawk. Brebeuf's stronger **frame** succumbed to his more deadly wounds in less than four **hours.**

" In their divine repose," writes their biographer, "they **say,** 'We passed through fire and water, but Thou **hast** brought us into a wealthy place.'"

The skull and other relics **of** Brebeuf, with **a** silver bust of the martyr, I have seen at the Hotel Dieu at Quebec. They are *said*, **by** superstitious devotees, **to** have wrought miracles of healing, as well **as** the conversion of the most obstinate heretics;* but a more potent spell is that of his lofty spirit, his earnest life, and his heroic death.

The night which followed this deed of blood was **a** night of terror at Ste. Marie, situated only six miles **distant from** St. Ignace. All day long the smoke **of the burning** village of St. Louis was visible, **and** Iroquois scouts prowled, wolflike, near the mission walls. All that night and

---

" Plus opiniastres."—Mercier, *Relations*, 1365, 26.

the night following the little garrison of forty Frenchmen stood at arms. In the chapel vows and prayers without ceasing were offered up. The Hurons rallied, and attacked the Iroquois in furious battle. But their valour was unavailing; they were, almost to a man, cut off. The Iroquois in turn, panic-stricken, fled in haste, but not without a last act of damning cruelty. Tying to the stake at St. Ignace the prisoners whom they had not time to torture, they fired the town, retreating to the music, delightful to the savage ear, of the shrieks of human agony of mothers and their children, husbands and their wives, old age and infancy, wreathing in the fierce flames' torturing embrace.* The site of the hapless town may still be traced in the blackened embers, preserved beneath the forest growth of over two centuries.

The mission was wrecked. The Hurons were scattered. Their towns were abandoned, burnt or destroyed, and themselves fugitives from a wrathful foe. "We are counted as sheep for the slaughter," piously writes Ragueneau. The Fathers resolved to transfer the missions to the Grand

---

* "Prenans plaisir à leur depart, de se repaistre des cris espouuantables que poussoient ces pauvres victimes au milieu de ces flammes, ou des enfans grilloient à ocstés de leurs mères, ou un mary voyoit sa femme rostir auprès de soy. —Ragueneau, *Relation des Hurons*, 1649, 13.

Manitoulin, where they might gather again their scattered flock free from the attack of their enemies. They unhappily changed their destination to Isle St. Joseph, now known as Christian Island, (probably from tradition of its Jesuit occupation), situated about twenty miles from Ste. Marie, and two or three miles from the mainland. They set fire to the mission buildings, and, with sinking hearts, saw in an hour the labours of ten years destroyed. On a rude raft, near sunset on the 14th of June, they embarked, about forty whites in all, with all their household goods and treasures, and, after several days, reached Isle St. Joseph. They built a new mission-fortress, the remains of which may still be seen. Here by winter were assembled six or eight thousand wretched Hurons, dependent upon the charity of the mission. The Fathers had collected five or six hundred bushels of acorns, which were served out to the perishing Indians, and boiled with ashes to take away their bitter taste. But the missionaries found compensation in the thought that man shall not live by bread alone; and they sought unweariedly to break unto the multitude the bread of life as they had it. In their extremity the famishing creatures were fain to eat the carrion remains of dogs and foxes, and, more horrible still, even the bodies of the dead.

O, the long and dreary winter
O, the cold and cruel winter !
O, the wasting of the famine !
O, the blasting of the fever !

Hungry was the air around them,
Hungry was the sky above them,
And the hungry stars in heaven
Like the eyes of wolves glared at them !

Before spring, harassed by the attacks of the Iroquois and wasted by pestilence, half of the number had died. Day by day the faithful missionaries visited the sick, exhorted the living, absolved the dying, and celebrated the sacraments in the crowded chapel, which was daily filled ten or twelve times. Night by night, in frost and snow and bitter storm, through the livelong hours the sentry paced his weary round.

During the winter the Iroquois ravaged the mainland, burning villages and slaughtering the inhabitants. St. Jean, a town of some six hundred families, which had hitherto resisted attack amid the fastnesses of the Blue Mountains, not far from the present town of Collingwood, was taken and destroyed. Here Pere Garnier, the scion of a noble family of Paris, shared the tragic fate of Daniel, the first martyr of the mission. He was slain in the act of absolving a dying Indian. With the opening spring the pinchings of hunger drove the starving Hurons from Isle St. Joseph to the mainland. **The** relentless Iroquois were awaiting **them. Of the large** party **who** crossed but **one** man escaped **to** tell the **tale of** blood. The whole country was a land of horror, a place of massacre.* There was nothing but despair on every side. More than **ten** thousand Hurons had **already** perished. Famine **or** an enemy more **cruel** still **everywhere** confronted them. They resolved to **forsake** their country, and **to** fly to some distant region in order **to escape** extermination by their foes. Many of them besought **the** Jesuits **to** lead them **to** an asylum beneath the guns **of Quebec, where they** might worship God in peace. The Fathers "consulted much together but more with **God,"†** as they expressed it, and engaged in **prayer** for **forty** consecutive **hours.** They resolved to abandon the mission. Dread of the Iroquois hastened their retreat.

"It was not without tears," plaintively writes Ragueneau, "that **we left** the country **of** our hearts and hopes which, already **red** with the blood **of our** brethren, promised **us a** like happiness, **opened for us** the gate of heaven.‡ **The** zealous

---

* "N'estoit plus qu'une terre d' horreur, et un lieu de massacre."—Ragueneau, *Relation des Hurons*, 1650, 22.

† "Nous consultions ensemble, mais plus encore avec Dieu."—*Ib.*

‡ *Relations*, 1650, **26.**

toil of fifteen years seemed frustrated, but, with devout submission the Father Superior writes, "whom the Lord loveth He chasteneth." They were accompanied in their retreat by three hundred Christian Hurons, the sad relics of a nation once so populous.* Along the shores where had recently dwelt eight or ten thousand of their countrymen not one remained.† The little band of fugitives sought refuge on the Island of Orleans, near Quebec. But even here they were pursued by the undying hate of the Iroquois, who again and again attacked the mission beneath the very guns of the fort. The remaining Hurons were dispersed in scattered groups far over the bleak Northern wastes from the Saguenay to the Mississippi, and soon disappeared as a distinct race. One band sought the aid of the powerful Ojibways, and confronted their merciless foe on the shores of Lake Superior, where a great battle was fought on the spot still known as Iroquois Point, otherwise, "the place of the Iroquois bones." A few families, the remnant of the once powerful Huron nation, still linger at Lorette, near Quebec.

Of pathetic interest is the specimen of the Huron language given in the *Relations* for the year

* "'Tristes reliques d'une nation autrefois si peuplée.'"—*Relations*, 1650, 26.

† "Il n'en restoit pas mesme un seul."—*Ib.*

1641. This language, once the vernacular of a numerous and powerful nation, is as completely lost as that of the builders of Babel. In all the world is none who comprehends the meaning of those strange mysterious words. Like the bones of the dinornis and the megatherium this meagre fragment is the relic of an extinct race—the tombstone over the grave of a nation. Yet the labours of the Jesuit missionaries have not been altogether lost. The lives of these devoted martyrs and confessors, notwithstanding the gross errors of their creed, were a perpetual self-sacrifice and self-abnegation. Through their efforts, also, multitudes of degraded savages were reclaimed from lives of utter barbarism and pagan superstition and cruelty, to the dignity of men and not unfrequently to the piety of saints. "It is well for the Protestant of to-day," says Dr. Whedon, "occasionally to go back on the path of history and form fresh acquaintance with the men of God who lightened up the night of the distant past. It intensifies our feeling of human brotherhood. It gives us a salutary consciousness of our communion with the Church general in all times and nations and sects. The chain of saints is a chain which stretches through *all* the ages." He who reads the story of the self-denying lives and heroic deaths of these Jesuit Fathers, although of alien race and diverse belief, however mistaken he may deem their zeal or however false their creed, will not withhold the throb of sympathy for their sufferings and of admiration for their lofty courage and unfaltering faith. The falsehoods and corruptions of their religious belief were an inheritance from the dark ages of superstition. Their inextinguishable desire to preach the Gospel, as they possessed it, to the perishing heathen, and their faithfulness in what they believed to be the call of duty, even unto a martyr's death—these spring not from the errors of Romanism, but from that incorruptible germ of Divine truth which even those errors could not utterly destroy.

DR. COKE. THE FATHER OF METHODIST MISSIONS.

"See how great a flame aspires,
 Kindled by a spark of grace;
Jesus' love the nations fires,
 Sets the kingdoms on a blaze.

'When He first the work begun,
 Small and feeble was His day;
Now the word doth swiftly run;
 Now it wins its widening way.
     —*Charles Wesley.*

THE especial characteristic of Methodism is its missionary zeal. It remembers the exhortation of its founder, not only to go to those who need it, but to those who need it most. It delights to remember the forgotten, to succour the neglected, to seek out the forsaken. As if prescient of the destined universality of the Church which he planted, John Wesley with prophetic soul exclaimed, "The WORLD is my parish."

On many a field of sacred toil have the ministers of the Methodist Church vindicated its title to the distinction of being pre-eminently a missionary Church—amid the cinnamon groves of Ceylon, in the crowded bazaars or tangled jungles of India, among the teeming populations of China, beneath the feathery foliage of the tropic palm in sunny islands of the Southern Seas, in the Zulu's hut and the Kaffir's kraal, and beside the mighty rivers which roll in solitary grandeur through the vast wilderness of our own North-West. With a prouder boast than the Roman poet, they may exclaim, "What place now, what region in the world is not full of our labour?"* In every land beneath the sun this grand old Mother of Churches has her daughters fair and flourishing, who rise up and call her blessed. The Sabbath chant of her hymns engirdles the earth with an anthem of praise, and the sheen of her spires rejoices in the light of a ceaseless morning.

To no man does Methodism owe more its missionary character than to the Rev. Thomas Coke, D.C.L. This marvellous man, of puny form but of giant energy, with a burning zeal kindled at the altar of eternal truth, like the angel of the Apocalypse flying abroad under the whole heaven with the everlasting gospel, preached the glad evangel of God's grace in both hemispheres; became the founder of Wesleyan missions in the East and West Indies, and the first bishop of the American Methodism—a Church now boundless as

* "Quis jam locus, ...
Quæ regio in terris nostri non plena laboris?"
— *Virg. Æn.* vv. 463, 464.

the continent—and after crossing eighteen times the stormy sea, was at last buried in its depths, whose waters, like his influence, engirdle the world. The study of this heroic life will be fruitful at once in lessons of gratitude to God, of inspiration to duty, and of zeal in the service of the Divine Master.

Nestling in the soft valley of the Usk, surrounded by the towering mountains of Wales, lies the old ecclesiastical borough of Brecon, the site of an ancient Dominican priory, whose ivy-mantled walls form one of the most picturesque ruins in Britain. In the oak-roofed, time-stained town hall of the ancient borough, at the middle of the last century, might have been seen, arrayed in the robes and insignia of office, a worthy alderman dispensing justice to the rural litigants of the neighbourhood. This was the chief magistrate of Brecon and the father of Thomas Coke. The future apostle of Methodism, unlike many of its early ministers, was the heir of a large patrimony. He was born three years before the middle of the century, 1747, and spent his early years amid the romantic surroundings of "Usk and Camelot," the scene of the legendary exploits of King Arthur and the Knights of the Round Table. In his sixteenth year he was registered as gentleman-commoner at Jesus College, Oxford. Among his college associates were the future Lord Eldon, Chancellor of England, who always retained for him a warm friendship; William Jones, who became the first Orientalist of his age ; Wharton, the historian of British poetry ; and the future bishops, Horne and Kennicott.

The handsome young patrician student was not proof against the seductions of Oxford society. He unhappily fell into evil habits, and even became infected with the infidel principles which were then too much in vogue at the University. But a divine restraint and guidance prevented him from making shipwreck of his hereditary faith and confirmed him in, at least, an intellectual apprehension of the truths of Christianity, although, as yet, he knew not experimentally their saving power. He completed his college curriculum with distinction, and shortly after his coming of age was elected to the chief magistracy of his native town. But, yearning to live a life of active beneficence, he entered holy orders in the humble rank of a village curate. Yet his heart was ill at ease, for he felt that the Saviour whom he was called to preach was to himself unknown. Still his moral earnestness awakened much interest in his parish. His church became crowded, and to accommodate the increased congregation, he erected a gallery at his own expense. During this time he made the acquaintance of Thomas Maxfield, Wesley's first lay preacher, and by him was led to more spiritual views of religion. He became increasingly diligent in the discharge of parochial duty. He met one day in his pastoral visitation, a humble Methodist farm-labourer, who, unlettered in the lore of the schools, was wise in the knowledge of God. From this rustic teacher the Oxford scholar gained a clearer acquaintance with the way of salvation by faith than from the learned divines and bishops of the first university of Europe.

The zeal of the popular curate soon began to exceed the bounds of clerical decorum, as regarded in the Church established by law. He preached with increasing fervour, and without the "regulation manuscript." He held special religious services out of church hours, and on week-evenings, in remote parts of his parish. He introduced the singing of the soul-stirring hymns of Watts and Wesley. He was no longer the easy-going cardplaying parson of his early incumbency, but a "dangerous fanatic," righteous over-much, and, in fact, infected with the pestilent heresy of Methodism, whose Arminian doctrines of free grace he proclaimed from the parish pulpit. The over-earnest curate was soon dismissed by his rector, admonished for his "irregularities" by the Bishop of Bath and Wells, and soon expelled from his church. His churchly notions were still so exalted that, after a long and profitable correspondence with a dissenting minister, when invited to a personal interview he would only consent to its taking place upon the neutral ground of a neighbour's house, his scruples preventing him visiting a dissenter or meeting one under his own roof. To receive himself the obnoxious brand of a Methodist was therefore particularly distasteful. He had just obtained his highest academical degree—that of Doctor of Civil Law. Ecclesiastical preferment was proffered him by a nobleman of powerful influence. But the authority of conscience was paramount, and he faltered not for a moment in his supreme loyalty to the convictions of his soul. Neither worldly hopes nor ignoble fears could make him swerve from what he deemed the path of duty.

A personal interview with John Wesley convinced Dr. Coke that for scholarship and saintliness the despised Methodists possessed the very paragon of clergymen. Mr. Wesley thus records his impressions of the young Doctor of Law:—" I had much conversation with him, and a union then began which, I trust, shall never end."

The zealous curate soon experienced the brunt of persecution. The sentence of his expulsion from the parish church was abruptly announced at the close of the morning service in the presence of the congregation; and, by a preconcerted scheme, as he passed out of the door the bells rang out a dissonant peal—a sort of ecclesiastical rogue's march- by way of valediction to the expelled pastor. Cider barrels were broached and a general rejoicing at his expulsion took place. To a man of his keen sensitiveness and churchly sympathies the indignity must have been poignantly felt.

But the expelled pastor could not be restrained from proclaiming the message of salvation committed to his care. The next Sunday he preached in the street near the church, immediately after the morning service, and announced that he would preach again the following Sunday. He was warned that it would be at the peril of his life if he did. "To render these menaces more significant," says his biographer, "sundry hampers of stones were brought to the spot, like a park of artillery drawn up on a field marked out for battle." But the Doctor, with that heroic courage which characterized him to the end of his life, was not to be daunted by an exhibition of brute force. He was sustained also by the presence of friends, who stood by him in this hour of peril. Among these were a Miss Edmunds and her brother, whose hearts had been touched by the evangelical preaching of the persecuted pastor. The brave girl stood on one side of him and the brother on the other. Their undaunted bearing cowed the craven spirits of the mob, who shrank from their premeditated assault and possible murder; and, like Paul before Felix, the feeble unarmed man spoke words of power which made his persecutors tremble.

Notwithstanding this rude initiation into evangelistic work, Dr. Coke not for a moment hesitated in his purpose. He resolved to cast in his lot with the despised and persecuted Methodists and to espouse the toils and hardships of the life of an itinerant preacher. He therefore, in 1777, made application to Mr. Wesley for admission to the Conference. That judicious man did not at once grant his request, but gave him time for consideration, while he made him the companion of his journeys and the sharer of his labours. Dr. Coke visited the Bristol Conference, and his desire became intensified to be numbered with those godly men entirely consecrated to the work of spreading Scriptural holiness throughout the land. Wesley yielded to his wish and wrote in his journal: "I went to Taunton with Dr. Coke, who has bidden adieu to his honourable name and determined to cast in his lot with us." He was soon preaching in the Old Foundery, London, at Seven Dials, and to immense multitudes of eager listeners in the public squares. Providence was opening for him a wider career than addressing a few rustics in an obscure hamlet. He was to become a mighty missionary organizer, whose beneficent influence was to be felt on earth's remotest shores to the end of time.

Wesley was now in his eighty-first year, and the care of all the churches and his vast correspondence was a burden which he gladly shared with this energetic son in the gospel, now in the vigour of his thirtieth year. He used to say that Dr. Coke was his right hand. The zealous preaching of the young evangelist often provoked the attacks of mobs. As he stood in the public square of Ramsbury, Wiltshire, he was assailed with sticks and stones, and his gown torn to shreds. The vicar of the parish, who headed the riot, bethought him of a more ingenious expedient. "Bring out the fire-engine," he shouted; and the preacher and congregation were soon dispersed by a few volleys of "liquid artillery." It was noticed as a remarkable coincidence, that within a fortnight that very engine proved powerless to suppress a conflagration which destroyed a great part of the village.

In the course of his itinerations, Dr. Coke revisited his former parish, from which he had been so heartlessly expelled. But the simple rustics found that they had lost their best friend, and welcomed him back with joy. The bells that rang him out chimed merrily at his return. He preached to two thousand people, who flocked to hear him from all the neighbouring villages, and wept over them, as the Saviour wept over Jerusalem. From that day the despised Methodists had a foothold in the parish, and soon after the Doctor had the pleasure of building a Methodist chapel where he had been cast out of the Established Church.

In his somewhat impulsive zeal, Dr. Coke arraigned Joseph Benson and Samuel Bradburn, first by correspondence and then before the Conference, for a presumed tinge of Arian heresy. Their orthodoxy being triumphantly vindicated, the Doctor magnanimously asked permission to publicly beg pardon for his offence, and was thus publicly reconciled.

In the celebrated Deed of Declaration, Mr. Wesley vested in the Legal Hundred all the authority of the Connexion. Dr. Coke was accused of influencing the choice of this " centurion band." Mr. Wesley, however, completely exculpated him by the laconic defence—" *Non vult, non potuit.*— He would not if he could, he could not if he would," and assumed the personal responsibility of the choice.

Dr. Coke was soon to enter upon what might be called his foreign missionary work. We have previously described the providential planting and progress of Methodism in America.* On the second day of September, 1784, John Wesley, feeling himself providentially called of God thereto, solemnly set apart by imposition of hands, Dr. Thomas Coke, to be Superintendent of the Methodist Societies in that country. Into the controversy to which that act gave rise, we shall not now enter. Suffice it to say, that the extraordinary development of American Methodism, under episcopal jurisdiction, seems a providential vindication of his procedure. In three weeks Coke, with his companions Whatcoat and Vesey, were on their way to America. The voyage was stormy and tedious, but he redeemed the time by study. He refreshed his classic lore by reading Virgil in a little nook between decks, and remarks in his journal: " I can say in a much better sense than he—

> " Deus nobis hæc otia fecit,
> Namque erit ille mihi semper Deus." †

---

* *Worthies of Early Methodism*,—Barbara Heck and Francis Asbury.

† " God has provided for us these hours of retirement,
And He shall be my God forever."

He laboured zealously for the conversion of the sailors, on shipboard, and believed that God had given him at least one soul as his reward.

He forthwith began ranging through the continent from Massachusetts to Georgia, a true bishop of souls, feeding the flock scattered through a primeval wilderness. Not unfrequently was he exposed to the novel perils of fording swollen rivers or crossing rugged mountains. Some of his escapes from imminent danger were very narrow. He met with prejudice and opposition in the western wilds as well as in an English parish, and records being excluded from a dilapidated church to which, nevertheless, cattle and hogs had free access. He preferred the rugged grandeur of the Blue Ridge Mountains to any other part of America, it was so much like his native Wales. He bore his testimony boldly against the sin of slavery, and provoked thereby much persecution. One lady offered a mob fifty pounds if they "would give the little Doctor a hundred lashes." Many emancipated their slaves, but others became more virulent in their opposition. In company with Asbury he visited General Washington at Mount Vernon, to seek his influence in favour of negro emancipation. But, their Master's business requiring haste, they could not accept an invitation to lodge under the presidential roof. During his seven months' visit he greatly consolidated and strengthened American Methodism, and laid the foundation of Cokesbury College, the pioneer of its grand educational system.

The importance of foreign missions was not then felt in the Churches of Christendom. When Carey, at a meeting of ministers, urged the duty of giving the gospel to the heathen, the President exclaimed, "Sit down, young man, sit down. When God pleases to convert the heathen He will do it without your aid or mine." But already Coke was meditating the vast missionary enterprises which are the glory of the Methodist Church. He opened a correspondence with India and Africa, and visited the Channel Islands as a key to missionary operations in France. The first field for the extension of the gospel, however, that seemed indicated by Providence was Newfoundland, Nova Scotia, and Canada. Thither in 1768, Dr. Coke and three fellow-preachers were sent by the English Conference. The voyage lasted thirteen weeks and was almost one continued tempest. The sails were rent, the timbers strained, and, half a wreck, the vessel sprung a leak, and falling on her beams-end, threatened instant death to all on board. The superstitious captain, attributing his disasters to the presence of the black-coats, exclaimed, "There is a Jonah on board, a Jonah on board." Rushing to Dr. Coke's cabin, he threw into the sea his books and papers, and seizing the diminutive Doctor, threatened to throw him after them if he were caught praying again. The passengers were put on short rations, and worst of all, the Doctor thought, the supply of candles gave out, so that his hours of study were curtailed. He solaced himself till he lost his books, with reading French, Virgil, and "every day a canto of the English Virgil, Spencer." "With such company," he continues, "I could live comfortably in a tub."

The project of reaching Halifax had to be abandoned, and running before the storm, they reached, on Christmas Day, the port of Antigua, in the West Indies. It was indeed a happy day for the sable myriads of those islands, for it brought them a glad evangel of redemption—of peace on earth and good-will to men. As Dr. Coke walked up the street of the town, he met a ship-carpenter and local preacher, John Baxter by name, who had under his care a Methodist Society of near two thousand souls, all blacks but ten. How came this native Church in this far-off tropic isle? Twenty-eight years before, an Antigua planter, Nathaniel Gilbert, heard John Wesley preach at Wandsworth, in England. The good seed took root in his heart and he brought the precious germs to his island home, where they became the source of West India Methodism, which, in turn, was one of the chief means of negro emancipation, and the beginning of the great movement of African evangelization. On the death of Nathaniel Gilbert, a pious shipwright took charge of the native Church, which eight years later was found so flourishing.

Dr. Coke ranged from island to island, sowing the seed of the Kingdom in the good and honest ground of those faithful African hearts. On every side he found evidence of the quickening power of the leaven of Methodism conveyed by strange means to those scattered islands—by converted soldiers or sailors, by pious freed negroes, and at St. Eustatius by a fugitive slave whose ministry was a marvel of spiritual success. Under the preaching of this black apostle, many of his hearers fell down like dead men to the earth, and multitudes were converted from their fetish worship to an intelligent piety. The Dutch officials of the island, however, scourged and imprisoned Black Harry, and passed an edict inflicting thirty-nine lashes on any negro found praying. With a fidelity worthy of the martyr ages, these sable confessors continued steadfast amid these cruel persecutions. Dr. Coke subsequently interceded at the Court of Holland for the religious liberty of the blacks, but, for the time, in vain. Yet he lived to see St. Eustatius a flourishing Wesleyan mission, and, ten years after, met Harry Black a freed and happy man.

Again and again the indefatigable evangelist revisited these sunny islands, which seem to have possessed a strange fascination to his mind. And well they might, for no where has the success of missionary effort been more glorious. At Barbadoes, an Irish soldier recognized one of the missionaries as an old pastor, and in a transport of delight threw his arms about his neck. At Jamaica, Dr. Coke received some insults from a number of drunken "gentlemen," but persisted in his apostolic labour of teaching the Gospel. Persecution here, as elsewhere, fostered the growth of the Church. The chapel was attacked by a mob, the Bible was hanged to a gibbet, and the Methodists were hooted at by the nickname of "Hallelujahs" in the street. In Bermuda, John Stephenson, for preaching the Gospel to the negroes, was imprisoned six months and fined fifty pounds.

Soon the work of evangelization was extended to Grenada, Montserrat, St. Kitts, Nevis, the Bahamas, the Carib Islands, Hayti, and the distant Bermudas. Amid privations, pestilence, shipwrecks, and sometimes bitter persecution, the missionaries toiled on till a free Christian civilization took the place of slavery, superstition, cruelty, and barbarism. Among the devoted labourers in these interesting fields have been our own Dr. Wood, Dr. Douglas, Mr. Cheeseborough, and others well known in Canada. As a result of the work thus inauspiciously begun, Methodism now numbers in those islands twenty-seven missionaries and nearly twenty thousand members.

Dr. Coke was in America when he heard of the death of John Wesley. Overwhelmed with sorrow, he hastened home to England. He was soon associated with Henry Moore in the preparation of a Life of the patriarch of Methodism. An edition of ten thousand was published in March, and in two months cleared £1,700. A second edition was brought out in June.

The French Revolution and the fall of the Bastile inspired a hope that the barriers to the Gospel had been broken down. Dr. Coke and M. De Queteville, a Guernsey Methodist, proceeded to Paris to open, if possible, a mission. In that city of amusements and pleasure, where, as one of its own wits has said, four-fifths of the people die of grief,* they could only get a congregation of six persons, and were warned to

* Paris, ville d'amusemens, des plaisirs, où les quatre cinquièmes des habitans meurent de chagrin.—Chamfort, *Caractères et Anecdotes.*

depart or they would be hanged on a lamp-post. They felt that the opportunity for the evangelization of France had not yet come.

Dr. Coke had been requested by the English Conference to prepare a Commentary on the Holy Scripture. On his fifth voyage to America he devoted himself with assiduity to the task. "I find a ship a most convenient place for study," is his rather exceptional experience, "although," he adds, "it is sometimes a great exercise for my feet, legs, and arms to keep myself steady to write." Proceeding from New York to St. Eustatius in company with the sainted "Bishop" Black of Nova Scotia, he found the vessel exceedingly loathsome from the filthy habits of the crew, yet he was able, he said, to become a contented Hottentot, and the consolations of God superabounded. He found the Methodist missionary in jail for preaching the Gospel and Negro women publicly flogged for attending a prayer-meeting. The penalty for the second and third offence of preaching was banishment and death, but the imprisoned missionary still preached through his grated windows to the Negroes without who listened with tears flowing down their cheeks. The Doctor might well denounce these cruel laws as rivaling the edicts of the pagan emperors of Rome. He zealously interceded with the Dutch and English

Governments for the cessation of these infamous laws, and eventually with success. In Jamaica he preached the first sermon ever heard in the town of Falmouth, although it had had for years a parochial clergyman with a handsome stipend. As he declared the necessity of the new birth, a sea captain exclaimed, "Sir, if what you say be true, we must all be damned. I don't like your doctrine at all," and the sermon was continued amid tumult and confusion. On his return to England his ship was chased by a French privateer, but was rescued by the appearance of Lord Hood's fleet.

The publication of Wilberforce's evidence concerning the slave-trade was to the heart of Dr. Coke an appalling revelation of the horrors of that "sum of all villanies." He therefore, in his yearning pity for the dark continent of Africa, projected a mission colony to that unhappy country, then seldom sought but for purposes of cruelty and crime. The expedition sailed for Sierra Leone in 1796, but, although the pioneer of successful missions, was itself a failure.

The same year he again embarked to attend the General Conference at Baltimore. Travelling now-a-days has lost much of the adventure and peril and discomfort it had in the last century. He describes the ship as a "floating hell" and the ill-treatment of the captain as too infamous to describe. He believed he wished to cause his death, out of hatred to Methodism. With a single shirt in his pocket, and refused the request for a little bread and pork, although he had paid eighteen guineas for his passage, Dr. Coke left the vessel in Chesapeake Bay in a small half-decked schooner, on whose bare deck he slept all night. With much privation and vexatious delays, travelling by boat, on horseback, or on foot, he reached Baltimore just in time for the Conference. *En route* he was joined by a Methodist preacher from beyond the Alleghanies, who had been lost sixteen days in crossing the mountains. His horse had perished and he himself had nearly died of the agonies of famine. Such were some of the episodes of the itinerancy eighty years ago.

On Coke's succeeding voyage the vessel was captured by a French privateer and confiscated with all the Doctor's baggage except his private papers. He was landed at Porto Rico, with scarcely raiment enough for his personal necessities, but escaping the horrors of a French prison, he at length found his way to Conference " on a borrowed horse with a great boy riding behind him."

During the terrible insurrection of "'98" in Ireland, Dr. Coke was in that distracted country, frequently exposed to personal peril, but providentially protected. It was a Methodist class-leader in Dublin who gave warning of the outbreak, and thus saved the capital from capture and pillage by the insurgents. The horrors of this civil war, for such it was, have never been fully recorded. A French invasion was invited by the rebels, and attempted under General Huburt. In cabins, in turf heaps, in peat mosses, pikes were concealed for the massacre of the Protestants, Beacon fires flashed the signal of the rising from peak to peak. Infuriated priests instigated the mob from the parish altars. The houses of the Protestants were burned, their cattle harried, and multitudes of non-combatant men, women, and children were cruelly massacred. Tens of thousands of armed ruffians, maddened with whiskey and fanaticism, ravaged the country with fire and sword. The air was tainted with the stench of thousands of unburied dead. Thirty-seven thousand of the marauders encamped near Ross, and the next day seven thousand were slain in a conflict with the royal troops. The Methodists, especially the itinerent preachers, were, for their loyalty, particularly obnoxious to the rebels, and several were cruelly piked with aggravated barbarity. During the reign of terror the Irish Conference met, through the influence of Dr. Coke with the Lord Lieutenant, in the city of Dublin. "O God, shorten the day of our calamity," it wrote, "or no flesh can be saved." With the magnanimity of a Gospel revenge, that very Conference set apart Charles Graham and James McQuigg as Irish evangelists, who, subsequently joined by Gideon Ouseley, preached and prayed and sang the Gospel in the Irish tongue into the hearts of thousands of their fellow-countrymen. Dr. Coke, it was, who proposed the measure, pledged its pecuniary support, and obtained for the missionaries the protection of the military authority. Soon after, he organized the missions among his Welsh fellow-countrymen, and had the happiness of seeing multitudes thereby brought to a knowledge of the truth. Two years later he formed a plan for the Home Missions, which have carried Methodism to the remotest hamlets of the island, and eight men were designated to destitute parts of England unreached by the regular circuits.

Two continents were now contending in friendly rivalry for his services. Alternately president of the English and American Conferences, his presence seemed so manifestly needed in both countries that he was continually crossing the ocean on his missionary voyages, as if either hemisphere were too narrow for the mighty energies of his large heart. At last the American General Conference of 1800 yielded to the request of the British Conference to allow Dr. Coke to remain in England. "We have, in compliance with your request" it wrote, "lent the Doctor to you for a season, to return to us as soon as he conveniently can, but at furthest by the meeting of the next General Conference." Only once more was he permitted to visit his American brethren, to whom he was endeared by most sacred ties and who mourned his death as that of the "greatest man of the eighteenth century." *

Amid the many wanderings of his active life, Dr. Coke found leisure for much literary work, as even the busiest may do if he will only improve his spare hours,—the *horæ subsecivæ*, which many think not worth trying to save. Among his useful writings are his History of the West Indies, in three volumes, octavo; five volumes of records of his missionary journeys; a history of philosophy, and numerous occasional pamphlets, sermons, and the like.

His *opus magnum*, however, was his Commentary on the Scriptures, begun by request of the Conference in 1789 and finished, after nine years' labour, in 1807. It reached the somewhat portentous size of six quarto volumes, splendidly

* *Vide* Asbury's Journal, May 21, 1815.

printed on the University press. The book, however, was not a success. It was probably too costly for the times, and was superseded by the more popular work of Dr. Adam Clarke. Disappointed at its failure, he offered the entire edition, worth at trade price £10,000, to the Conference for £3,000. This offer was accepted, and he bade farewell to literature for the more congenial field of misionary toil.

With redoubled zeal, as the years fled by, he traversed Great Britain from end to end on behalf of his Irish, Welsh, and Home Mission enterprises. He threw himself with vigour into the then novel work of promoting Sunday-schools and the temperance reform. The spiritual necessities of the soldiers and sailors of Great Britain, of whose trials and temptations, virtues and vices he had seen so much during his wanderings, lay like a burden on his heart. At length, in 1804, a Methodist missionary and his wife were sent to the Rock of Gibraltar. They were well-nigh wrecked in the Bay of Biscay, and driven to the Barbary coast. Reaching at last their destination, it yielded them only the asylum of a grave. Yellow fever wasted the little community, and the missionary and his wife soon fell victims to its power. An infant daughter survived, who, adopted into the family of Dr. Adam Clarke, became the wife of a Methodist minister and the mother of the distinguished Dr. James H. Rigg, now President of the Wesleyan Conference. But the historic Rock was not abandoned; and a succession of faithful missionaries, of whom were our own Dr. Stinson, and our living townsman, the Rev. Mr. Cheeseborough, have ministered to the wants, temporal and spiritual, of multitudes of England's gallant redcoats, among them several hundred Canadian youths, of the Hundredth (Prince of Wales) regiment, quartered at Gibraltar.

The unhappy condition of the French sailors and soldiers, pent up in the prison ships of the great naval depots, also appealed strongly to that loving heart whose sympathies were as wide as the world. In the Medway alone was a prison population of 2,000; and altogether in England not less than 60,000, crowded into unventilated and often infected ships. Sometimes the friendless, hopeless, and often half-naked wretches sought escape from their despondency by suicide. The Rev. Wm. Toase, the father of French missions, gained admission to the hulk *Glory*, and preached to the prisoners in their own language till forbidden by the commissary. Dr. Coke hereupon appealed to the Earl of Liverpool, and obtained permission to have preaching at all the naval stations, with characteristic generosity meeting the enlarged expenditure himself. Through this exhibition of love to our enemies, many French prisoners—among them some of noble rank—carried back to their native land not only kindly recollections of their "hereditary foe," but Christian fellowship in that kingdom which embraces all races of men. William Toase had also the honour of planting in France that Methodist Church which has survived the overthrow of successive dynasties and is contributing greatly to the moral regeneration of that lovely land.

At length Dr. Coke was permitted to see the successful inauguration of an African mission, the precursor of subsequent glorious moral victories among the Kaffirs, Hottentots, Fingoes, Bechuanas, Zulus, and other tribes of that benighted land. On the abolition of the slave trade, the British Crown established in Sierra Leone the colony of Freetown, as an asylum for stolen Negroes rescued from re-captured slave ships. Here, in 1811, four volunteer missionaries were sent. Nowithstanding the more than decimation of the missionary ranks by the deadly climate, the work has been maintained, till in thirty chapels assemble more than twenty thousand native Methodists who have abandoned their vile fetichism for a pure spiritual worship, and five thousand children crowd the mission schools.

We now approach a romantic episode in the already venerable missionary's history. The flower of love, like the night-blooming cereus, blossomed late in his life; but its beauty and fragrance were all the more grateful to his lonely heart. He was in his fifty-eighth year. His brow was bronzed by eighteen transatlantic voyages and by sojourn beneath a tropic sun, and his once raven hair was silvered by time. In his busy life he had never found leisure for courtship and marriage. But now in its quiet eventide, he found the solace of communion with a kindred spirit in the tenderest and most sacred of earthly relationships.

The growing claims of the vast and increasing missionary enterprises of the Church called for active efforts for their support. Dr. Coke not only exhausted his own large patrimony in their aid, but "toiled," says his biographer, "from day to day like a common mendicant." While at Bristol on a begging tour he was introduced to a Methodist lady of large fortune, who subscribed for his mission two hundred guineas. The generous gift led to an acquaintance, which, in time, resulted in the union of their hearts and lives and fortunes for the glory of God and the salvation of souls. "Unto Thee, O God," wrote the lady on her wedding day, "we give up our whole selves,—all we have and all we are,—to thee wholly and entirely."

But marriage made no change in the soul-absorbing pursuits of the zealous missionary organizer. He seemed to feel that the time was short, and it remained that they that have wives be as though they had none. He continued to travel, preach, write, and beg with unintermitted energy. His devoted helpmate was not long permitted to aid with her love, her sympathy, her fortune, which though ample, was unequal to her liberality, her noble husband. After six years of married life, he was again left alone in the world. His heart, sore-stricken by her loss, having tasted the solace of domestic happiness, again sought an aftermath of joy in a second marriage. But in a few days from the anniversary of the wedding day, he was again left solitary. "With the presage," writes his biographer, "that these bereavements had been designed to leave him the more untrammelled for the tasks that might remain, he dedicated himself afresh *to God alone*. Henceforth he would think, preach, write, labour, and pray more fully than ever for one object,—the extension of Christ's Kingdom among men."

And faithfully he performed his vow. He was now about to inaugurate his last and greatest missionary enterprise. For many years the spiritual destitution of India had lain heavy on his heart. On the banks of the Indus, where the foot of an

Alexander had faltered, a merchant's clerk had conquered an empire. With three thousand troops, on the plains of Plassey, he routed an army of sixty thousand, with the loss of only two and twenty men, and laid the foundations of our Indian Empire of 200,000,000 souls. But though open to English commerce, India, by the decree of the Company of Leadenhall Street, was closed to Christ's Gospel. But "India," wrote Dr. Coke, "still cleaved to his heart; he could give up all for India." Parliament, wrote Wilberforce, was especially "set against granting any countenance to Dissenters or Methodists in favour of sending missionaries to India." Dr. Coke, therefore, rather than fail in his long-cherished purpose, was willing to go in his character as a clergyman of the Established Church, and as such offered his services. For this he has been censured, as if self-seeking and ambitious, and disloyal to the Church in whose service he had spent forty years of his life. The prudence of his course may well be questioned; of a hallowed ambition for the salvation of souls, he is certainly gloriously convicted; but of sordid self-seeking he was absolutely incapable. "He was already," writes Dr. Stevens, "wielding an episcopal power compared with which an Indian see would be insignificant." Salary, he sought not, only permission to spend and be spent for India.

The proposition, however, was not accepted. But Dr. Coke's faith and zeal and courage were not to be overcome: Ceylon, "the threshold before the gate of the East," was more accessible than India; and thither he was determined, by God's grace, to go. Friends remonstrated against a man in his sixty-sixth year, worn with toil and heavy cares, braving the perils of a long sea voyage and residence in the torrid zone; but it was in vain. "I am now dead to Europe," he wrote, "and alive to India. God Himself has said to me, 'Go to Ceylon.' I am so fully convinced of the will of God, that methinks I had rather be set naked on the coast of Ceylon, without clothes and without a friend, than not go there.—I shall bear all my own expenses, of course," he adds. He eagerly began the study of Portuguese, which was largely spoken in Ceylon; and which he subsequently prosecuted on shipboard to the day of his death. The letter just quoted was written from Ireland, and he sought first the sanction of the Irish Conference to his purpose. Revering him as an apostle, and almost as the father of Irish Methodism, it supported with enthusiasm his project. Fired by his example, Gideon Ouseley begged with tears to be allowed to accompany him; but his providential work was too manifestly at home for the Conference to grant its permission.

Dr. Coke now sought the sanction of the English Conference. Unmoved by their fears for his health, he declared that "their consent, he believed, would add years to his life; while their refusal would infallibly shorten his days." "Many rose to oppose it."—We quote the narrative of Dr. Stevens.—" Benson, with vehemence said it would 'ruin Methodism,' for the failure of so gigantic a project would seem to involve the honour of the denomination before the world. The debate was adjourned to the next day. Coke, leaning on the arm of one of his missionaries, returned to his lodgings in deep anguish, the tears flowing down his face in the streets. He was not at the ante-breakfast session the next day. The missionary hastened to his chamber, and found that he had not been in bed; his dishevelled silvery locks showed he had passed the night in deep distress. He had spent the hours in prayer, prostrate on the floor. They went to the Conference, and Coke made a thrilling speech. He not only offered to lay himself on the altar of this great sacrifice, but, if the Conference could not meet the financial expense of the mission, he offered to lay down thirty thousand dollars toward it. Reece, Atmore, and Bunting had already stood up for him, and Thomas Roberts made for him a 'moving appeal.' The Conference could not resist longer without denying its old faith in the providence of God. It voted him authority to go and take with him seven men, including the one for Southern Africa. Coke immediately called out from the session Clough, the missionary who had sympathized with him in his defeat the day before, and walking down the street, not now with tears, but with joy beaming in his eye, and with a full heart, exclaimed, 'Did I not tell you that God would answer prayer?'"

Among the missionaries who accompanied him was William Martin Harvard, who, after five year's residence in India and Ceylon, became subsequently superintendent of missions in Canada, residing for ten years at Montreal, Quebec, Toronto, and other important Connexional centres.*

Soon the missionary band assembled at Portsmouth for embarkation, Dr. Coke having first made his will and bequeathed all his property to the fund for aged and worn-out ministers. The Sunday before sailing, he preached his last sermon in England, from the text, "Ethiopia shall soon stretch out her hands unto God." With prophetic faith he exclaims, "It is of little consequence whether we take our flight to glory from the land of our nativity, from the trackless ocean, or from the shores of Ceylon.

* He died in England, 1837, aged sixty-seven years.

> I cannot go
> Where universal Love not shines around;
> And where He vital breathes there must be joy!"

Like this are the exultant words of the monk, Jerome, in the fourth century: "Et de Hierosolymis et de Britannia æqualiter patetaula cœlsetis." *

> Not from Jerusalem alone
>   The path to Heaven ascends;
>   As near, as sure, as straight the way
>   That leads to the celestial day,
>   From farthest climes extends
> Frigid or Torrid Zone.

"On the 30th of December, 1813," continues the narrative of Dr. Stevens, "they departed in a fleet of six Indiamen and more than twenty other merchant vessels, convoyed by three ships of war. Coke and two of the missionaries were on board of one of the Indiamen, and the rest of the party on board of another. All were treated with marked respect by the officers and the hundreds of troops and other passengers who crowded the vessels. In about a week a terrific gale overtook them in the Bay of Biscay, and a ship full of people, in which Coke had at first designed to embark, was lost. On the tenth of February one of the Indiamen hoisted her flag at half-mast; all the fleet responded to the sad signal: the wife of Ault, one of the missionaries, was dead, and

---
* Heironymus—*Ep. ad Paulinum.*

that evening was buried in the sea. She died 'triumphant in the faith.'

"Severe gales still swept over them, especially at the Cape of Good Hope. Several sailors were lost overboard, and the missionaries suffered much in their health. The fleet did not touch at the Cape, but McKenny was borne thither by one of the ships. In the Indian Ocean Coke's health rapidly declined. On the morning of the third of May his servant knocked at his cabin door to awake him at the usual time of half-past five o'clock. He heard no response. Opening the door he beheld the lifeless body of the missionary extended on the floor. A 'placid smile was on his countenance.' He was cold and stiff, and must have died before midnight. It is supposed that he had risen to call for help, and fell by apoplexy. His cabin was separated only by a thin wainscot from others, in which no noise or struggle had been heard, and it is inferred that he died without violent suffering. Consternation spread among the missionary band, but they lost not their resolution. They prepared to commit him to the deep, and to prosecute, as they might be able, his great design. A coffin was made, and at five o'clock in the afternoon the corpse was solemnly borne up to the leeward gangway, where it was covered with signal flags; the soldiers were drawn up in rank on the deck; the bell of the ship tolled, and the crew and passengers, deeply affected, crowded around the scene. One of the missionaries read the burial service, and the moment that the sun sunk below the Indian Ocean the coffin was cast into the depths."

In his last letter written a few days before his death, Coke earnestly asks for additional missionaries, sketches his work in Ceylon and India, and anticipates tracing the work of "that holy and celebrated man, Francis Xavier."

The missionaries with heavy hearts proceeded on their voyage and after a passage of twenty weeks reached Bombay. But God raised them up friends and opened the way before them. On reaching Ceylon they were hospitably lodged in the Government House. Lord Molesworth, the commandant, who, with his troops, attended the first service, was so deeply impressed by the sermon that he left a dinner party to kneel in prayer with the missionaries till he found peace in believing. Soon after, returning to England, his ship was lost with all on board save two or three. While it was sinking, he walked the deck, pointing the terrified passengers to the Saviour of men. Embracing Lady Molesworth in his arms, they sank into the waves, locked in each other's arms, and thus folded together in death they were washed ashore. Such were the first fruits of the Methodist mission in Ceylon. Another trophy of that first sermon became the first native missionary to Asia. Many of the priests also believed. One of these introduced Mr. Harvard, afterward our Canadian superintendent, into a temple, where, in front of a great idol, he preached from the text, " We know that an idol is nothing in the world, and that there is none other God but one." The good work rapidly spread, till in 1876, the last Report at hand, there are in Ceylon 58 missionaries and assistants, 200 preaching-places, and over 3,000 Church members.

The death of Dr. Coke was the beginning of a new era in the history of Wesleyan missions. Auxiliary societies were organized with a central committee, which has become the most vigorous propaganda in the world of the Christian religion among the heathen. In Ceylon, in India, in China, in South and West Africa, in the West Indies, in Australia and Polynesia, multitudes of degraded and superstitious pagans have been raised from most abject depths of degradation to the dignity of men and prepared for the fellowship of saints. And this glorious result is in large part the monument and memorial of the life and labours of DOCTOR THOMAS COKE, THE FATHER OF METHODIST MISSIONS.

www.ingramcontent.com/pod-product-compliance
Lightning Source LLC
Chambersburg PA
CBHW031450160426
43195CB00010BB/922